A Glimpse of Glory

A Glimpse of Glory

GONVILLE FFRENCH-BEYTAGH

edited by
Vera Hodges

Darton, Longman and Todd
London

First published in 1986 by
Darton, Longman and Todd Ltd
89 Lillie Road, London SW6 1UD

Reprinted 1986

ISBN 0 232 51691 X

British Library Cataloguing in Publication Data

ffrench-Beytagh, Gonville
  A glimpse of glory.
  1. Prayer
  I. Title
  248.3′2   BV210.2

  ISBN 0–232–51691–X

Phototypeset by Input Typesetting Ltd, London SW19 8DR
Printed and bound in Great Britain
by Anchor Brendon Ltd, Tiptree Essex.

Contents

Foreword

This is a book based on talks by Canon Gonville ffrench-Beytagh. Many people, in this country and in Africa, have found him an outstanding teacher of prayer, with a deep understanding of the mysteries which he tries to make visible, and also of the people who come to learn. Again and again he has been urged to publish his talks; but there are no prepared scripts for he speaks from brief notes or from none at all. A certain amount of team work has gone into this attempt to bring his thoughts to paper; friends have contributed their memories, their transcripts, and their tapes, and it has fallen to me to sort through a wealth of material and plan this book.

Part 1 is based on my own notes of a retreat given by Gonville in the late autumn of 1984. He gave us copies of George Herbert's sonnet 'Prayer' and used it to structure his meditation. T. S. Eliot has likened that sonnet to John Keats' nightingale which

Charm'd magic casements opening on the foam
Of perilous seas, in faery lands forlorn.

But for Gonville and for some of us it opened no casements on 'faery lands forlorn' but, rather, it opened windows in heaven; one looked through them to see a glimpse of glory, and from them to see earth's problems in a new light. Herbert calls prayer 'the soul's banquet', and I felt the whole experience deserved that title. We sat round in a cool chapel on dank December days to feast with Herbert and Gonville; and Ezekiel and Julian of Norwich and St John the Divine were also of the party. Prayerful, imaginative Christians have often excelled, like the psalmists and prophets before them and like Jesus their master, in putting their wisdom into pictures and poetry. Gonville constantly echoes the Bible and the great spiritual writers and adds much striking imagery of his own, as he sees the remission of sins reflected in black holes in space or the love of the Trinity in the Victoria Falls.

Part 2 is largely drawn from the notes of some who heard him at his parish church, St Vedast, and elsewhere. Lancelot Andrewes, in one of his sermons preached before King James 1, speaks of preachers whose words are lit from the tongues of fire at Pentecost; and, for some hearers, he says, their words may come 'like red-hot iron that burns into wood leaving a mark that will be there for always'. For many, Gonville's words have left that mark which will be there for always. Of course it was not only the words which burnt deep: there was the sense of prayer behind them and the vigorous, human, often humorous, manner in which they were spoken. We can only hope that something of his personality will shine through his words here and the reader will catch a little of the awareness of God's presence and power which he is able to convey.

VERA HODGES

Acknowledgements

This book has been constructed out of a considerable number of talks, sermons, and retreat addresses that I have delivered over recent years. The fact that it has become a book at all is due in the main to two people. The first is Alison Norman who managed to sort out the bits that seemed to have more than just an ephemeral value. The second – though not in order of importance – is Vera Hodges who undertook the mammoth task not only of finally collating, selecting and concocting it into a book, but did all the typing and final preparation of the script on her word-processor. Without those two there would have been no book and I am deeply grateful to them both. I must also add my thanks to Lesley Riddle and her assistants at Darton Longman and Todd for their patience and their meticulous final editing.

But there are many others to whom I owe my thanks: to Barbara Waite who first started to tape some of my talks in Johannesburg, to Barbara Price and Doreen Woolfenden who carried on doing so here in England. These ladies have also done a great deal of typing over the years, as have a number of other people, specifically Pia Gibbons (as she then was). Laura Clayton, Madeleine Barry, and Christopher Graham did some admirable work in legible longhand. Sisters of the Community of St Mary the Virgin at Wantage, and of the Community of the Sisters of the Love of God at Fairacres, Oxford, and many members of the Servants of Christ the King have also made contributions to the book. I thank them all and those others who have helped, not least by encouraging me to go on trying to get my thoughts, such as they are, into some sort of shape.

The quotation from 'Choruses from *The Rock*' from *Collected Poems 1909–1962* by T. S. Eliot is by permission of Faber and Faber Ltd.

GONVILLE FFRENCH-BEYTAGH

St Vedast-alias-Foster
London EC2

Biographical note

Gonville ffrench-Beytagh was born in 1912 in Shanghai, the son of an Irish business man. ('Beytagh' is an Irish name pronounced like 'beater'.) His parents separated, and when he was nine he was sent to England in the care of a woman teacher who became his guardian. He went to Monkton Combe School and Bristol Grammar School. When he was sixteen he went to New Zealand to join an agricultural school, but he was quickly expelled after a midnight escapade. He ran away from the job which was found for him and, at the age when most future ecclesiastics are studying for examinations at school or university, Gonville was bumming round New Zealand as a tramp and casual labourer, getting into fights, dodging the police, milking cows, and shearing sheep.

He had lost contact with his family, but an unexpected meeting with a relative led to help for a passage to South Africa. There he was out of work for a period but eventually found a job in an office in Johannesburg. There he met Toc H and gave some help to their boys' clubs; but he was an irreverent agnostic and kept apart from the religious side of their life.

The home in Shanghai had been completely pagan, and the churches which Gonville had met in England had led to a determination never, of his own will, to attend another. The turning point came when he was attacked by muggers in a subway and received a blow, probably from an iron bar, which broke his jaw. One of his Toc H friends – Alan Paton, the author of *Cry, the Beloved Country* – at once came to see him in hospital. Gonville had to stay there for some time, and this gave him opportunity (as Alan Paton put it) 'to reflect on the nature and destiny of man and the nature and lack of destiny of himself'. What sort of person did he want to be? Had the lively Christians whom he had met through Toc H more to show him than the carefree, adventurous, Bulldog Drummond types whom he had previously admired? When he came out of hospital he began to attend services. He was barely a Christian when he knew that he must be a priest. He talked to Bishop (later Archbishop) Geoffrey Clayton, who was to become a great friend and influence, and some substitute for the close family which he had never known. A year after leaving hospital he joined St Paul's Theological College in Grahamstown.

Gonville resented the restrictions of life in the theological college but stuck it out with impatience. He was ordained in 1939 and served in several places in the Diocese of Johannesburg. There is ample evidence of the deep influence of his ministry as a parish priest. For a time he was chaplain of a sisterhood while acting as Diocesan Missioner and doing more administrative work than he enjoyed. In 1955 he was invited to Rhodesia as Dean of Salisbury Cathedral.

In 1965 he went back to Johannesburg as Dean of St Mary's Cathedral. He had gradually come to see South Africa's apartheid system as utterly unchristian and he was determined to show his people that it was contrary to God's love, and to bring black and white together, at least in his cathedral. He pleased some and enraged others. He faced petty persecution and, in January 1971, he was arrested and charged with subversion under the South African Terrorism Act. After a long trial he was convicted and sentenced to five years imprisonment; but the sentence was quashed on appeal.

It seemed clear that he would not be allowed to continue working in South Africa, but he saw that he could serve the country by lecturing and writing about the true nature of apartheid. His book *Encountering Darkness* gives his view of the system with which he clashed. He was already an Honorary Canon of Johannesburg and in 1973, after settling in England, he was made an Honorary Canon of Canterbury. For a short period he was an assistant priest at St Matthew's, Westminster, and in 1974 be became Rector of St Vedast-alias-Foster, a church in the City of London.

Part One

GOD'S BREATH IN MEN

Prayer

Prayer, the Church's banquet, Angels' age,
  God's breath in man returning to his birth,
  The soul in paraphrase, heart in pilgrimage,
The Christian plummet, sounding heaven and earth;
Engine against the Almighty, sinner's tower,
  Reversèd thunder, Christ-side-piercing spear,
  The six-days' world transposing in an hour,
A kind of tune, which all things hear and fear;
Softness, and peace, and joy, and love, and bliss,
  Exalted manna, gladness of the best,
  Heaven in ordinary, man well drest,
The milky way, the bird of Paradise,
  Church-bells beyond the stars heard, the soul's blood,
  The land of spices; something understood.

GEORGE HERBERT (1593–1633)

1

About ourselves

I want to talk to you about God; but first I want to talk about you and me. Each of us is unique, not just physically unique with our own fingerprints and blood patterns, but inwardly unique. No one else has exactly your fears and hopes, your failures and successes, your loneliness and loves. You are you and there never has been and never will be anyone just like you. You are unique, irreplaceable and, to that extent, a very important person. You may not carry as much clout as the Prime Minister or the President of the USA but you are as important in the total scheme of things as any other person who has ever lived. The South African catechism from which I learnt my faith begins, 'God made me for himself'. He did not make you for your parents, or for your husband, or your wife, or to be a clergyman, or to be anything else. He made you because he had a delight in the sons of men. You may question his taste, but he wanted and designed you for himself. It amazes me when I think of the myriads of beings God created and realize that I am unique and made by God for himself.

Understanding the process of human conception as we do, I don't think we can believe that each one of us is individually designed to a specification laid down by God. We are designed by that statistical thing, random selection. But you may remember that poem by Keats about stout Cortez when he first climbed over the mountains and looked at the Pacific:

> when with eagle eyes
> He stared at the Pacific – and all his men

Looked at each other with a wild surmise –
Silent, upon a peak in Darien.

It seems to me as if at the moment of my conception and your
conception, heaven stood still. (Though it is always still, for
there is no time there.) Then your forefathers, those who have
gone before you, and God, and his angels, all joined for a
moment of 'wild surmise'. Who is he going to be? What is she
going to be like? Is this going to be the kind of person I long
for him or her to be?

I and you are made in the image of God. Not as a replica
of God. Not as an imitation of God. An image – as we learnt
in physics long ago – is a reflection in a mirror. You are made
to reflect God. And the whole creation that groans and travails
is a vast mirror with a myriad facets set at a million angles, and
you and I are each irreplaceable facets of that mirror. Only
when, together, each individual light truly reflects God, will
that mirror send back the perfect likeness. Then redemption
will be achieved. In the meanwhile each of us can reflect a little
of the glory and love in God's eyes when he looks at us. Of
course, though I was made for God's image, through my sins
and other people's sins, I have become this rather horrible
thing, me; but however much I have deformed and distorted
and defaced the image, I still remain God's. I am *capax dei*,
capable of God, made to be filled with God.

Michael Ramsey said, 'In me there is a God-shaped emptiness.' Nothing else will fit it. And the Psalmist bears winess:
'Like as the hart desireth the water-brooks: so longeth my soul
after thee, O God.' And: 'My soul hath a desire and a longing
to enter into the courts of my God.' I have felt a hypocrite
saying that; I don't always desire and long for the courts of
God – but my soul does. That is what the soul is made for and
it does long to be filled with God. And it is in answer to that
deep longing that you are here. However near to God you may
be there is still this longing and emptiness.

That desire and longing which we have for God is a complementary longing: it answers the yearning which God has for
me and God has for you. It may not be theologically defensible,

but I think it is true to say that there is a you-shaped emptiness in God. His longing is shown in the Old Testament – 'O my people, what have I done unto you? Wherein have I wearied you?' 'What have I done to make you go away?' 'All the day long I have stretched out my hand to a disobedient, a gainsaying people.' And Jesus himself said in Jerusalem: 'How often would I have gathered thy children together even as a hen gathereth her chickens under her wings, and ye would not.' And at the Last Supper he said: 'In my Father's house are many places . . . I go to prepare a place for you.' I go to get ready your place for you; it is your place which you can't share with anyone else.

I am God's and he is mine for ever. God's longing for us is answered by our much more feeble yearning and longing for him. His longing and our longing come together: that is what religion is about. Julian of Norwich sees the spiritual life in two aspects: the first is us seeking God, the second is 'the beholding'. When we have sought God he reveals himself and we can behold him. She says, 'the seeking pleaseth God'. You are seeking God, so you have already pleased him. 'The seeking pleaseth God,' she says, 'but the beholding pleaseth the soul.' If God reveals himself that will please you enormously. Then she says, 'the seeking is as good as the beholding'. We may never see him, but the seeking will go on and that is as good as the beholding.

You are not drawn to God primarily for your own benefit but for his. I find that in what I have learnt about prayer from the Little Sisters of Jesus. Their rule is based on Charles de Foucauld's spirituality. They have an hour of prayer which is an hour for God, just for God. They taught me how to spend that hour by a very simple formula: 'Look, Lean, Long, Love.' Simply look towards God, not straining, just looking and listening. Any words that come to you can be turned over gently while you are leaning towards God and longing. It is not like Eastern forms of contemplation in which one waits passively; we move towards God, we look, and lean, and long. You can use the verse of a Psalm or some other phrase to help you, but just keep yourself leaning and longing. The end of the prayer is loving. You cannot reach that loving by yourself. It always has to be given to you by God himself. Keep looking and leaning towards God and in his own good time you will know the touch of love.

2

About God

In this chapter I want to speak to you about God. I feel like a man aspiring to enter the Chinese civil service in the days when the entrance examination consisted of being put in a room with wads of paper and told to write down all that you knew about everything. I cannot speak coherently because God is unspeak-.able. Studdert Kennedy called him the 'Unutterable Beauty'. He is the ineffable, the eternal absolute, the beyond, the wholly other, beyond sight and hearing. He is the source of all being. He is the substance of all being. He is the sustainer of all being. What he says of himself in the beginning is 'I am'; that is who I am. He just is and there is nothing at all apart from God. 'I am Alpha and Omega, the beginning and the end.' I am the totality of all things. Julian of Norwich goes on repeating, 'I it am.' God is everywhere, or as one mystic puts it, 'There is nowhere where God is not.' There is no thing in which God is not. Because he is beyond speech, we cannot describe him; we can only stammer. The Psalms go on about God with much repetition because there is nothing to say except to turn over the concept of his totality. He is beyond hearing, yet we do hear echoes of him. Lovely art and great music and lovely words give us echoes of him. He is beyond sight, yet we do catch glimpses of him.

One must find for oneself some way of thinking about God. My own favourite concept in the last few years has been the statement made by Rudolph Otto and used by Michael Ramsey. God is *mysterium tremendum et fascinans*. The word *mysterium* is loosely translated as 'mystery' but it does not mean a puzzle; it means a secret. Now a secret is something precious to me which I give you in a moment of confidence, and you must not tell it to anyone else. But the *mysterium* of God is not something that you must not talk about; it is something that you cannot talk about because he is beyond speech, beyond hearing. The mystery cannot be told; it is so precious it cannot be disclosed.

The Psalmist says of God: 'He hath made darkness his secret place' and 'clouds and thick darkness cover him'. It is a warm, comforting darkness, a darkness where we are at home, not a frightening darkness. And he has to make the cloud and darkness to cover him to shield us from his blinding, brilliant, blazing glory. It would blast us out of existence unless he covered himself and shielded us from his transcendent, trinitarian majesty. He hides himself and I know his secret is beyond my understanding.

Let us look at this concept of God, '*mysterium tremendum et fascinans*'. *Tremendum* comes from the root which gives us 'tremendous' and refers to the tremendous, monumental, majesty of God, immovable and unchanging. Most people sense this in mountains; even pagan mountaineers find that the mountains give them a perception of something other. In the Bible, Mount Sinai, Mount Hermon, Mount Tabor are places of spiritual power. Mount Athos has that special atmosphere for the Greek Church. For most people mountains seem to speak of the tremendous, massive, ageless power of God.

I have never been able to feel that and I often wondered why. It wasn't until I was about seventy that I realized that it might be because I am depressive and inward-looking, and slow to respond to visual beauty. But several years ago I had an experience which heightened my perception of this aspect of God, of his power and majesty and might and glory. I was in America and I saw the Grand Canyon for the first time. Unbelievable! One mile deep into the depths of the earth! There the chasm stands as it has stood undisturbed for millions and millions of years. Its layers and layers of stone have lain there since long before man was born. It's like a mountain upside down. People like me are most likely to encounter God in the depths. I felt that sense of totally solid majesty and unchanging power down there in the Canyon, though I can't see it up there on the mountain.

The word *tremendum* suggests the objective might of God; it also suggests our subjective reaction to his might. It suggests the word 'tremble', as in that negro spiritual:

> Were you there when they crucified my Lord?
> Sometimes it causes me to tremble . . .

We tremble at the presence of God, but not with fear. It is a trembling at the anticipation of love. We tremble with wonder at the revelation of God.

And the other word is *fascinans*. Fascinate means to beguile, to lure, to hypnotize, to draw in. God is longing to draw us in and into himself. There is the same idea in the word 'numinous'. *Numen* means presence, the presence of God. The verb *nuo* means 'I nod' or 'I beckon', and a numinous place is a place where God draws you, beckoning you nearer to himself. There are numinous things like the Blessed Sacrament and the Bible: in both these things God is drawing us and wanting us. And there are numinous places. I had my first inkling of this when I was about nine. I was brought up by two completely pagan parents (we never had Christmas in our house). We lived in Shanghai, but my mother was born in Japan and we used to go there for our holidays. There is a Buddhist shrine at a place called Nara. I didn't know about God but I had a sense there of – I didn't know what. I understood it better twenty years later. Walsingham, or Julian's cell at Norwich, or Glastonbury – these are numinous places. Though God is everywhere, there are places where he is more easily discernible, more available. Some churches are like thin places in the atmosphere between heaven and earth. There are places where we feel that he is drawing us to himself. And there are numinous people too.

The same idea of *mysterium* is in another Latin phrase which I have always loved, *deus absconditus*, from Isaiah 45:15: 'Verily thou art a God that hidest thyself.' I like Meister Eckhart's words: 'Suppose a man hiding and he stirs, he shows his whereabouts thereby. God is the same. No one could have found God at any time, but he gave himself away.' He gave himself away first at the burning bush. He revealed himself again to Ezekiel. He gave himself away to John on the Island of Patmos and quite certainly he gave himself away to you: you wouldn't be reading this unless he had given himself away to you somehow. He gave himself away in the total self-giving of the incarnation. God hides himself but he gives himself away in countless ways.

The other thing I want to speak about is the glory of God. The glory is the manifestation of the presence of God. In the Bible the Hebrew word for this is *kabhod*. The Greek word which we translate 'glory' is the word *doxa* which gives us 'doxology'. The word *doxa* misses the concept of majesty which was conveyed by the word *kabhod*. The trouble with *doxa* is that it is a Greek word, and the Greek idea of glory was a shining, flimsy, airy-fairy characteristic of gods and goddesses who cavorted round in heaven up to no good. It was a dazzling idea of glory but the power and majesty were not there. The Jew has an idea of the shining brightness of God in his word *shekinah*. As the sabbath evening comes on they light the candles and say that at that time the *shekinah* descends on every Jewish household. It is the orthodox Jew's word for the bright cloud of glory. That bright *shekinah* idea has crept into the Bible word glory. But *shekinah* is not a biblical word; it is a rabbinical word which only came into use after the Old Testament had ended.

Of course the dazzling glory of God is there throughout the Bible. The story of the transfiguration shows his shining glory. Christ's face and his clothes were blazing blindingly, dazzlingly bright and there was a bright cloud surrounding him. In Genesis God says, 'Let there be light,' and the primordial light of God himself is there before the creation of the sun and moon and the stars. This kind of light is beyond our imagination. Persil may wash whiter than white, but the light of God is lighter than light! The primordial light is the reflection of the uncreated glory which one day we will see in the City where there is no need of the sun and the moon, for the glory of the Lord will lighten it and the Lamb is the light thereof, and there shall be no night there. All that is in Revelation, and Christ himself (in

John17:3) refers to 'the glory which I had with thee before the world was'. Though this glory is beyond our conceiving, it is not beyond our glimpsing. The light of the presence of God was there at the burning bush; the sight of the glory of God was like a devouring fire on the top of Mount Sinai; it accompanied the tabernacle in the wilderness, in the cloud by day and the pillar of fire by night.

Moses gat him up into the mountain and he met God there in the midst of the cloud. Why is it that we don't recognise this more often? We look for him in brightness and beauty and joy; but we are just as likely to meet him in the cloud of doubt and depression and fear. People like me, who know the torment of depression, have a certain advantage: we are more likely to find him in the depths than we are to find him in the heights. We may see a glimpse of the dark glory of Calvary.

The Old Testament word for glory, *kabhod*, contains something beyond light which the Greek had no means of conveying. *Kabhod* is something entirely different. (The only way we meet it in the English is in the negative – the name Ichabod which means 'the glory has departed'.) Now *kabhod* literally means weight. It was used of a man of substance, a man who counted for something, a man whom we might look up to. So Solomon had *kabhod*; he had weight, substance, power and majesty. The verse, 'The mountains are moved at the presence of God,' suggests that the mountains had to move over to make room for the glory of God. Glory is not something diaphanous and flimsy but something totally solid and substantial. 'Tremble thou earth at the presence of God, the presence of the God of Jacob.' When God puts his foot down the mountains tremble at the tremendous weight and solidity and massivity of the great God. To me that concept is more real than the shining effervescence of some heavenly Daz. The glory of God is so solid that it can displace things like mountains.

There is a story of Romans who hoped to sack Jerusalem as they had sacked all the great temples of the East. They came to the Temple hoping for jewels and riches. They found nothing, no statues even. They had heard that in the centre of the Temple was the Holy of Holies and they thought that there they would find the hidden treasure. When they broke into the Holy of Holies they found there – nothing. There was no room for anything, it was filled with *kabhod*; it was filled with the solid glory of God's presence. The Hebrew felt that the presence of God had a dangerous power waiting to be unleashed. The high priest was allowed to go into the Holy of Holies once a year on the Day of Atonement. He walked in a cloud of incense, and round the bottom of his priestly robes were little bells so that when he moved round the people could hear that he was still alive in the terrible presence of God. That's how the Jewish people thought of *kabhod*, the great glory of God. And we may share their awe:

> Lord, thy glory fills the heavens;
> Earth is with its fullness stored;
> Unto thee be glory given,
> Holy, Holy, Holy Lord.

3

'Prayer'

'Prayer, the Church's banquet'

In the first two chapters I spoke about ourselves and then about God. Now we shall consider the dialogue between the two of us, between God and ourselves in prayer. We shall see how it was conceived by George Herbert and described in his poem 'Prayer'.

Herbert begins with prayer as 'the Church's banquet'. I think we are often too plodding and pedestrian in our prayer. That is an aspect of prayer, for we have a duty to pray come hail, hell, or high water, and sometimes for a long time it is a dutiful plodding along. But prayer can be much more than that, much richer and much fuller. The life of prayer is a banquet.

There is rich food available for us. There are books, especially the Bible and the spiritual writers of all the ages. There are many to choose from: old writers like St Teresa, St John of the Cross, Julian of Norwich, de Caussade; new ones like Thomas Merton and Father de Mello; in between them Evelyn Underhill and Baron Von Hügel. And of course the Bible is pre-eminent as the food of prayer, and specifically the Psalms. In the South African church they decided to put the 'damnatory clauses' in brackets so that we could leave them out, but I think we should keep the Psalms whole. They are strong meat, but they were Jesus' own prayers, the only prayer-book he had, and he knew them by heart. Besides the Psalms there are the great hymns. I think most of us build up our own anthologies of prayer which we like and feel that we can use.

These are parts of the food of prayer which is spread out for us in a great banquet.

It is important at a banquet not to try to eat the whole lot! Pick and choose what attracts you. We have our 'attraits' in prayer. In our attraits we differ from each other, and what attracts each of us is different at different times. Sometimes we are specially attracted by the mystery of God, or by his love or his power, or by the cross. God puts something in front of us and says, 'Now follow this for a while and it will lead you closer to me.' He beckons us, lures us with different rich things from the banquet, and we are stupid if we do not follow what attracts us and seems to draw us.

From time to time I have to go to banquets in the City of London where there are tables of food, golden goblets, gleaming glass and shining chandeliers and a suggestion of music and merriment. But prayer is not a City banquet; it is a royal banquet, the Banquet of the Marriage of the King of Kings. We are there not just as guests but as the heirs of the house, entitled to enter into the richness of the life of prayer and feed ourselves richly.

Don't be afraid to loosen up, to let down your hair. Don't be too stiffly British in your prayer. (Though there is nothing stiff in a Briton like Julian of Norwich with her lovely words about the blissfulness of prayer and God calling her 'my darling'. There is nothing stiff in Thomas Traherne or George Herbert himself.) I mean that if you always wear sensible shoes you will go plodding; you will not go dancing. There are times for silver slippers and rings on your fingers and bells on your toes. There is a time for lightness and brightness. There are times in prayer when God offers the lightness and brightness, when you can leap towards him instead of just plodding along. So 'the Church's banquet' refers to the prayer which is rich with all that you find lovely. There are times when prayer is different – we'll talk about that later on – but the more you can welcome the rich parts the better.

'. . . Angels' age,
God's breath in man returning to his birth'

Now for prayer as the 'Angels' age'. We talk about the Iron Age and the Bronze Age, eras when iron or bronze was the dominant material. Nowadays we talk about the Age of the Computer. The 'Angels' age' is the era, the area, in which angels are predominant. They are all about us. 'Therefore with Angels, Archangels and all the company of heaven' – we are never alone at prayer. Remember what 'company' means – *com panis*, 'with bread'. We eat bread with the angels; man eats angels' food. We are 'with all the company of heaven' – not just the company in heaven, for when we are at prayer we are companions with the dissident Russian Christian in the concentration camp or the forests of Siberia; we are with the Orthodox monk on Athos, with the Little Brothers of Jesus, with the Cowley Fathers, and with Christians everywhere. We are with the company of heaven eating bread with them all.

And 'Angels' age' reminds us that here we have no abiding city, no staying place. We are amphibious creatures; we belong in heaven as well as on earth. We belong in eternity as well as in time. Because we are amphibious creatures, prayer becomes a deep breathing of the soul which takes up gulps of the air of heaven, of the great Spirit of God. We can breathe the air of heaven which is our home. So prayer is 'God's breath in man returning to his birth' – his Spirit in us in returning to his birthplace, his origin from whence he comes, which is heaven. He is reaching out to return there.

We should not neglect one of the simpler concepts of prayer, the idea of coming home. Prayer means being relaxed, putting one's feet up, just being there, being where we know we are welcome. God always welcomes us when we turn to him in prayer. We are wanted by him and trusted. Prayer is coming to God with a sigh of relief as we leave the rush and hustle and hassle; or leave the places where we are not always wanted and are often rejected. We are coming home through our prayer.

And there is the biblical idea that our prayer is not just our

own activity. It is God's Spirit in us. He is praying and returning
to his origin. Prayer is the work, the activity, of the Holy Spirit
of God moving within us. 'God hath sent forth the Spirit of his
Son into our hearts, whereby we cry, Abba, Father' (Gal. 4:6).
He is crying: we are giving words to his cry. 'The Spirit himself
beareth witness with our spirit that we are the children of
God . . . The Spirit himself maketh intercession for us with
groanings that cannot be uttered' (Rom. 8:16,26). There is the
idea of the Spirit breathing within us, taking us along with him,
dragging us along even if we are unwilling. The Spirit is longing
to take us on the wings of the Dove into the presence of God.
In prayer we meet the Holy Spirit yearning and longing and
striving within us to unite us to God. For that purpose Christ
came to redeem us, to make it possible for us to be united with
God, and the Holy Spirit does the work of calling us, of dragging us along into the presence of God. And I think we are,
at our best, aware of this movement within us. At times we
are reasonably certain that our prayer is more than just what
we are doing ourselves.

This is all to do with what is called in theology the procession
of the Holy Spirit. 'He proceedeth from the Father and the
Son.' The word 'proceeding' sounds rather pedestrian, but the
Holy Spirit is not like some solemn verger plodding along in
front of a cathedral procession. The Holy Spirit is pouring,
cascading forth, in tumultuous torrents of love, pouring out
into the Son, pouring himself in torrents of love. And the Son
himself is joyously, gloriously, pouring back his love into the
Father. In this great procession of love pouring forth love, it
is the Holy Spirit who is poured forth, it is he who is cascading
forth in this glorious divine love affair. And that love is so
unlimited, so limitless, that it spills over.

The Holy Spirit spills over. This is not because God can't
contain himself but because he is so longing to share his life of
love and joy and glory that he has made us as containers. That
is what *capax dei* means – capable of containing God. Our
glory and our purpose is to be filled with the reality which is
God. We are designed to be filled with the love of God. We
are like the great tankers, filled with petrol or milk, that go

trundling along the road marked 'Capacity 20,000 gallons'. But you and I go about with a couple of gallons sloshing round in the bottom instead of being filled with the fullness of God. Yet that is what he made us for, that is the purpose of our existence – to be filled with God. If we think of prayer being for that, then we are expanding ourselves to receive a share of what is poured out and spilling over of the tremendous infinite power of the love of God.

I spoke earlier about the Grand Canyon in America as being for me a picture of the immovability and massivity of God; but I have an earlier picture, of the Victoria Falls in Africa, as a picture of the life of God. There is a lovely story in Ezekiel about how he sat by the river of Chebar. He sat there astonished for seven days. I once spent four astonished days at the Falls, being pounded into the ground by their deafening roar and the magnificent sight of the millions and millions of gallons every moment pouring out, cascading, thundering down into the gorge below. It seemed as if the Congo and Zambezi had drained all the water out of Africa and there it was. For me this made a picture of the ceaseless activity within the being of God himself. It was like the cascades of infinite divine love interflowing within the Godhead between the Father and the Son. God the Father is begetting love; God the Son is begotten love; God the Holy Spirit is the ceaseless flow of love between the Father and the Son. The Spirit binds them together in the gorgeous, ceaseless torrent of love.

And beside the Victoria Falls is the rain forest. It is a weird place where you can put on sou'wester, hat, oilskins, gumboots, and walk into the forest and you're just soaked to the skin. Water gets through everything. The heavy mist comes from the spray that rises up from the great canyon into which the torrent flows. It penetrates everything and seems wetter than ordinary water. As the mist from the cascade will drench us and soak into us if we put ourselves there in the forest, so, if we put ourselves close to the Lord God, his love that overspills and overflows will soak us in the Spirit. We long to share his love in as far as it can be shared by human beings. And he has made us for that, he has made us to be *capax dei*, to stand, as it were in the rain forest, to be drenched in the love of God. That is the spiritual life.

For me, the Canyon stands for the massivity and dependability of God, whereas the Falls make a picture of this torrential love of God which never stops. We are caught up into God's love in the prayer of the Spirit praying within us. And we are caught up with the prayer of all the ages and the prayers of all the saints and of our own forbears. We are in their prayers with the angels and the archangels. It is one great paean of love, agonizing sometimes, from the great chorus of heaven of which we are a part.

'The soul in paraphrase'

Prayer is 'the soul in paraphrase'. To paraphrase something is to express its sense in a different way. We bring out the richness of a phrase by putting it into our words. In prayer the soul is trying to express what is beyond expression. We can't fully express our experience of God; words cannot capture him. We can only stammer. Poets, using rhythm as well as words, can sometimes speak more clearly. Yet we need words and cannot do without them. Remember that the words we use in prayer are always used for our own benefit, so that we get our meaning clearer; God knows what is in our hearts without needing our words.

Martin Luther said an intelligent thing about words in prayer: 'The right method is to use few words but in many and profound senses. The fewer the words, the better the prayer. Few words with much meaning is Christian: many words with little meaning is pagan.' The fewer the words, the better the prayer; therefore in prayer we repeat words. Our Lord warned us against vain repetition, but a great deal of prayer is repetition; we've got to use it. It's not *mere* repetition; that would be vain magic. We take words and repeat them, letting them resonate like a gong or a turning-fork. The words are the surface-mechanism of a reverberation, an echoing, which gradually gets going deep down inside; they are a means of getting in tune with God.

This repetition sets up a reverberation in tune with the rhythms of all God's creation, with the sun and the moon and the stars and the tides, with my heart and your heart, and with the rhythm of all life. The psalms are full of repetition and of that reverberation.

We often find that our attempt to paraphrase, to find another phrase for something, gives us a paradox. We use terms which seem to contradict each other while in fact they are complementary. If God is the totality of all that is, he is so beyond everything that we have to look at him first from one aspect and then from another. We see different aspects which are coming into a whole; that's what a paradox is.

The first great Christian paradox is the doctrine of the holy, glorious and undivided Trinity. There are three Persons and one God. There's a hymn, which I don't care for, which goes something like, 'Three in one and one in three, Bewildered here we worship thee!' God is not 'three in one'. Three into one won't go. He is three Persons – in one category of being – and one God – in another category. And we hold those concepts together, as the Athanasian Creed spells them out: 'So the Father is God, the Son is God, and the Holy Spirit is God; and yet there are not three Gods but one God.' 'Where Jesus is,' says Julian of Norwich, 'there is the Trinity.'

The other great paradox is the incarnation. Jesus is wholly God – 'God of God, Light of Light, Very God of very God, Begotten, not made, Being of one substance with the Father.' He is all that, and he is totally man, 'tempted in all points like as we are'. And we have to hold these truths together. One thing you must never do is to try to resolve the paradox. When you try to do that you get over-simplifications – like the comparison of the Trinity to a shamrock, or Sunday-school pictures of the Son of God painted as an effeminate person in a white nighty with an incandescent glow behind him. If that is the incarnate Son of God I want no part nor lot with him. You can't resolve the paradox in a picture which tries to simplify the truth. We must look at our faith this way and that way, turning over in our thoughts mind-blowing words like 'For in him dwelleth all the fullness of the Godhead bodily.'

Holding to orthodoxy, said G. K. Chesterton, is like driving two wild horses together in a chariot; but you must hold both horses together, for that way you reach the truth. If you try to resolve the paradox you lose the dynamic tension of Christianity and it goes limp. Without the paradox you get a religion of blancmange and strawberry mousse – very nice perhaps, but not the truth.

And in prayer we must struggle to express and know many sides of the Christian paradox, as we think of Jesus in the Virgin's womb, see him in his mother's arms and on the wings of the wind, adored by angels, and dining with tax-collectors. Reason stands on tiptoe, reaching out to concepts beyond reason, for the totality of the incarnation is far beyond anything we can understand.

'. . . heart in pilgrimage'

Next, Herbert says that prayer is the 'heart in pilgrimage'. Prayer is going on and in to meet God. Sometimes we encounter him over there – the great transcendent God; sometimes we journey in to find him here – the great immanent God. The search for God and the search for self are often very much the same thing. Sometimes we stress the inner aspect of God and sometimes the transcendent, but together they speak of the truth.

'The heart in pilgrimage' – the spiritual life, the life of prayer, is not static. There is movement in it. I know a number of people who have been trained in 'transcendental meditation'. They do have a discipline; most of them do two periods of twenty minutes a day. It is a search for oneself in a way and without a real concept of God. But their search is less active than ours. For us prayer is not passive. You may remember St Augustine's phrase: 'Our hearts are made for thee and they are restless until they rest in thee.' The pilgrims have to go towards God until they find him and come to rest in him. Adoration is not a static act but a reaching out towards God. For me the pattern of adoration is a looking towards God, a listening for him, a leaning towards him and a longing for him, until there comes an experience of love.

Pilgrimage has one or two different aspects. There are the high spots, the joy, the fun and games and the banquet. There is also the other side of the pilgrimage: the sore feet, the uphill bits, the weary plodding on and on, the times when you turn a corner and there seems to be nothing there and no end in sight. And in those difficult times the best prayer – one of my favourite prayers – is a prayer of St Teresa: 'O God, I do not love thee. O God I do not even want to love thee, but dear God, I do want to want to love thee.' Put more loosely: 'O God, I don't want to be a hypocrite – I have never really loved you, but there are times, lots of times, when, somewhere deep down, I do really want to want to love you.' That rings true with me, and when it comes from St Teresa there is an authenticity about it. It is a prayer which I can pray when I can't pray any other kind of prayer.

'The Christian plummet, sounding heaven and earth'

There are two ways in which a plummet is used. A ship uses a sounding line to measure the height and depth of the water; the plumb-line is used to make sure that the wall of a building is straight. Prayer is the Christian plummet reaching down to the depths and up to the heights, and helping to keep things straight.

Think of the psalm:

> If I climb up into heaven, thou art there:
> If I go down to hell, thou art there also.

Climbing up into heaven is hard and going down into hell is dead easy. The road to hell doesn't go straight down; if it did we would see that it was dangerous and avoid it. The road to destruction is a broad one with roses all the way. We may slide down it seeing nothing wrong. For most of us the dangers do not lie in the notorious sins which bring their own punishment, as adultery may bring us to the VD ward or the divorce court,

and anger may lose us our friends and stealing may lose us our
jobs. We are probably brought down by more subtle faults,
like sins of omission.

Prayer has its heights and depths. People like me, depress-
ives, may encounter God more really through the depths and
darkness than in the heights. If you are really deeply depressed
you don't find God easily, or you wouldn't be depressed; but
when you come out of the darkness and look back, you realize
that God has been there all the time. You begin not to dread
the depression. You know it will come, for that is your lot; but
there is the knowledge that you will find God afterwards.
'Christ for the joys that were set before him endured the cross.'
It didn't make the cross light to bear but, for the joy of what
he anticipated, he endured it; and if you are subject to
depression you have to endure it.

In a period of reactive depression – the kind which most
people have – you will be depressed about many things, failure
among them. Priests are very conscious of their failure to get
the Christian message across, of failure to meet people's needs,
of rejection, of being betrayed, of people letting them down.
In all these depressing situations it is well to remember that
the passion was about failure and rejection and betrayal; so it
is possible in those times to make yourself identify with Jesus.
I can claim indentification, not because I am following my
Lord, but because I am no good. I am often not accepted, as
he was not accepted; so I am in good company.

That brings us to the prayer of anger or complaint. That is
a valid and necessary aspect of prayer: we should complain to
our Father if we feel that we have been given a raw deal. We
may feel that we lack education, or beauty, or brains, or
strength. If you feel like that, say so. Remember how the
Psalmist goes on about his troubles. 'The ungodly cometh on
so fast' – My God, why? Those are right and proper prayers
showing a right relationship of a child to his father. A young
mother was worried because her four-year-old son said, 'I hate
you. I wish you were dead.' That child was sound; he trusted
his mum and wasn't afraid that she would hit him. Because we
trust God we can complain to him. Some people think praise

is saying nice things about God. Sometimes we treat God as if he were a rather fierce dog who won't bite us if we pat him and tell him that he is a good dog. You can't pat God. That isn't praise, it is phoney. Praise is telling God what is in your heart. Sometimes it will be thanks and love, but sometimes it will be anger.

Remember the plumb-line aspects of the plummet. How can you tell that your prayer is going in the right direction, towards God? How can you judge if you have got the angle wrong? You can't really, but there are indicators which you can apply to the life of prayer. It is hard to judge a single hour of prayer. It may have been an hour in which we were totally distracted and yet went on trying to draw the mind back to God; Teresa would say that had been an hour of great value. But if we look back over a year or so of prayer I think there may be two indications. One sign is that if prayer is going right it does bring a sense of satisfaction – not satisfaction with yourself, that would be fatal – but a sense of being fulfilled and made complete. And the other sign is our Lord's own. He said, 'By their fruits ye shall know them.' One may look back after a year of prayer and ask, 'Am I slightly less bitchy? Am I slightly less anxious? Am I less touchy than I was?' The answers can indicate whether your prayer is moving in the right direction.

Engine against the Almighty, sinner's tower,
Reversèd thunder . . .'

This is a difficult passage but I am pretty sure about the picture in Herbert's mind. He imagines a siege with ancient engines of war – the battering ram, the catapult, the movable tower from which archers shot arrows over the wall. This gives us an image of persistence in prayer, especially in petition. Christ told the story of the woman who asked her neighbour to give her bread at midnight. She went on asking and achieved what she wanted. So also the importunate woman turned the mind of the unjust judge by her persistent pleading. Jesus' point was that 'men ought always to pray, and not to faint'. So we approach God

with much asking. We 'cry to him day and night'. We fling our
requests at God. We are the sinners on the tower who shoot
arrow after arrow.

'Reversed thunder' – I think what Herbert meant here was
that intercession may turn away some threatened or actual woe.
Thus Psalm 106 shows Moses defending the Israelites when
they deserved God's punishment:

> So he said, he would have destroyed them, had not Moses
> his chosen stood before him in the gap: to turn away his
> wrathful indignation, lest he should destroy them.

Moses stood in the gap turning back the thunder of God.
Another Old Testament image of intercession is that in Exodus
17 where Moses, holding up his hands on the mountain, defends
Israel against the Amalekites. Similarly our Lord stands
between us and the wrath of God. He 'reverses the thunder'
by 'standing in the gap'. Remember the hymn:

> For lo, between our sins and their reward
> We set the Passion of thy Son our Lord.

It is our part to try to reverse the thunder of the world's cry
of agony by opposing it with our prayers. There is a cry of
agony that goes up from the world unceasingly. It rises not
only from the Third World and its famine-stricken people but
from the derelict and destitute in our own society, from the
deformed in mind and body, and from those who bore them
and care for them. I hear very clearly the cries of agony that
rise up from the dying and the dispossessed and discarded
people from all round the world. I hear the whimper of desolation from those who are too weak to weep or to cry out.
Besides the cry of pain there is a scream of anger at the total
injustice and hopelessness of it all. The cry goes up all the time
from the earth to God. It is insistent and incessant, day in, day
out, through all the days of time. Millions are dying of starvation. Their agonized cry is, of necessity, the cry of non-faith.
How can you have faith when you are faced with certain death
for your child? It is a cry with no hope in it and with no faith
in it.

But there is another cry, the cry of faith which arises from the Church, and that cry needs to be as insistent and incessant as the cry of agony. We know from Our Lord's teaching that we do not always need great faith but only the mustard-seed of faith, and that is a great comfort to me. If I can bring my very little faith ('Lord I believe, help thou my unbelief') to lift up my prayer with the great stream of adoration which the Church lifts up to God, then I am at work for all the world. This great torrent of prayer and praise rises up from the world in many forms – in the Eucharist which is being celebrated somewhere in the world every hour of every day, and in the prayers which are said and sung by faithful people in the great religious houses, and in churches and homes. Wherever prayer is offered and by whomsoever and of whatever kind it may be, it has the intercessory function of becoming part of the cry of faith which mingles with the cry of agony and gives it the wings of faith. Just as an aircraft takes off into the wind and so obtains its lift, so the cry of faith lifts up the cry of agony, up to the throne of God.

Most of the world doesn't believe in intercession. The Muslims don't believe in intercession; for them fate is kismet, it is ordained. The Buddhists and the Hindus don't believe in intercession since, for them, through karma we are caught up in the wheel of destiny and there is nothing to be done about it. Only Christians believe in intercession. But we Christians are a small people. And how many Christians do this work of interceding, or even believe that it is worth doing? This does cast a tremendous responsibility upon us. Our cry of intercession must be as persistent as the constant cry of the world's agony.

I don't know whether Herbert would recognize that interpretation of 'reversed thunder', but I think of our cry of faith, our intercession, as countering and reversing the thundering cries of despair.

'Christ-side-piercing spear'

After that concept of the sinners' tower and the reversed thunder there comes another image of intercession: the 'Christ-side-piercing spear'. This is a magnificent concept. Remember the incident when Christ had died but they doubted the reality of his death. 'But one of the soldiers with a spear pierced his side, and forthwith came there out blood and water' – the precious blood and the water of life. The key word is that 'forthwith' – immediately there gushed forth the river of living water. It had been pent-up, dammed up inside him, despite his longing. His death is what releases the life. It is only when Jesus is dead that the water begins to flow.

This leads us to think of our Lord as the spring and source of all life, as the stream, the living waters of life. We can apply all the lovely Old Testament language: from Ezekiel comes the picture of the Church being a great river; wherever the river comes there life will grow. So from the sacred heart, in devotional thought, there pours out the water of baptism and the precious blood which we drink. As the soldier's spear was the agent which let out the pent-up love, so our intercession is the agent which pierces and frees the dammed-up love of God.

To me this is a very real concept. There is the limitless, unlimited, love and power of God. He longs to pour his love and his peace and his plenty upon the world. He suffers an agony of longing because he made us for himself, to love and glorify him; but we refuse his love. He left us free to respond as we would. In so far as he has given us free will, to that extent his own will is not free. In love of his creation he had to limit himself. We are his creatures and the priests of his creation; all the animals were brought to man. Man is the key factor in the creation and the key factor in releasing this power of God onto the earth.

You can think of God's will as a vast reservoir of love and peace and power, and every human being as a tap. Most of the taps are turned off: they are not bad, but they don't know, or don't care, or are selfish by nature as we all are. An intercessor is someone who turns his tap on so that the love of God can

begin to flow through. And if you love him – the more holy
you are – the more power and love can and does flow through.

We few, weak Christians need to be together in our inter-
cessions. One lovely aspect of the religious life is that all hours
of day and night – on Mount Sinai, on Long Island in New
York, and all the way round the world – religious communities
are making reparation and offering the Mass and the daily
offices. Constant intercession does go on and the love of God
does flow through. It is like freeing a passage through a dyke
which has dammed up the will of God. Take the stopper out
and the power of God begins to flow into his earth and flood
it.

The spear of intercession or petition is the prayer of those
who cry under any tribulation, 'Come unto me O Lord'. Each
of these cries is like a spear piercing God, but the spears need,
like the wings of an arrow, the wind of faith to lift them up.
Pre-eminently (to use the mystic's expression) if we want to
pierce the heart of God we have to do it with 'the dart of
longing love'. On the 'sinners' tower', where most of us stand,
words are immaterial; it is the dart of longing love which can
pierce God's heart so that his power is released.

Intercession is an integral part of prayer. Intercession, in so
far as it is that dart of longing love, is adoration. It is the
arrow-head of prayer. There are some people who think of
intercession as a lower form of prayer; they want to change
gear a couple of times and get up to some kind of airy-fairy
mystical experience of adoration. This is nonsense. We spoke
about attraits earlier; I know one person who is, I think, very
holy and her prayer, as far as I understand, is almost all intercession. That's what her work is. We don't know how God
apportions our tasks; some people do a great deal of intercession and some do it less directly. But it is not a lower form.
The Epistle to the Hebrews writes of what our Lord is doing
in heaven: 'He ever lives to make intercession for us.' You
couldn't find a higher vocation than joining in that intercession
with him.

We have many pictures of the risen and ascended and
glorified Jesus, Jesus as he is. I myself haven't a specially clear

concept of Jesus of Nazareth, the man of Galilee, as he was in
the time of the Gospels. I am more drawn to the glorious
pictures of him as he is, as in the Revelation. He is the lion
and the lamb – as paradoxically contrasted a pair as 'Arsenic
and Old Lace' – but they present two complementary aspects
of Christ. And he is surrounded with ten thousand times ten
thousand and thousands of thousands – what a brilliant phrase!
And all fall down before him and worship him. And I enjoy
the part where the elders take off their crowns as if they were
hats and throw them on the ground. And among these gorgeous
pictures: I saw 'a lamb as it had been slain' ruling on the right
hand of the Father. Christ is both the Lamb of God and the
high priest offering intercession.

If you want to know why it's necessary to offer intercession
– I don't know. I know from the Gospels that Jesus was quite
capable of walking past a blind man until the man called for
him. Then he turned and asked, 'What do you want me to do?'
He wanted the blind man to say, 'Lord, restore my sight.' Our
Lord needed the request and used it. We know that Christ
procured our redemption once for all upon the cross. There
he made 'a full, perfect and sufficient sacrifice, oblation and
satisfaction, for the sins of the whole world'. It was totally
done, there on the cross. But something more needs to be
done, and he is doing it in heaven as he makes intercession for
us. His work needs to be applied, and its power poured out on
the earth; and he still needs us to make our requests. That is
an important task of every Christian on this earth. Those people
who are ill, or bedridden and inactive, have perhaps a peculiar
vocation to intercession. They can use their own pain, their
inadequacies and their suffering and frustration, to make those
darts of longing love on behalf of the agonized world. Old age
and illnesses are given purpose when they set us free to set
free the dammed-up love of God.

'The six-day's world transposing in an hour,
A kind of tune, which all things hear and fear'

The 'six-day's world' is the weekday world. 'Six days shalt thou labour and do all that thou hast to do; but the seventh is the rest of the Lord thy God.' The Muslims keep every Friday. The Jews keep every Saturday. The Christians keep every Sunday. Seven days to the week and twenty-eight days to the month seems to be basic to the nature of things. There were two occasions in history when a ten-day week was tried, but it didn't work. It contradicts what we are, for we are made for a seven-day rhythm. Rhythm is important in life and an important factor in prayer, and rhythm is set in motion by repetition which reverberates deep down within us.

Repetition gets a rhythm going. An accepted method of affective prayer is to take a word or a phrase which you like the sound of and which has a full content for you. Take that word and sound it like a tuning fork. Hold it to your ear till the sound dies away, then repeat it. Sound your note slowly – every five seconds, every ten seconds, as you like, and this sets up the deep reverberation. This reminds me of the Orthodox idea that in prayer you may take your head down into your heart: there your intellectual concerns are simplified.

I don't know exactly what George Herbert is saying here, but prayer sets the tone, the note, either for the day or for the week. The tone for the day is best sounded in the morning. Jeremy Taylor said, 'I take it that every Christian that is in health is up early in the morning.' Morning prayer sets the tone for the day and Sunday, the sabbath rest, sets the tone for the weekday ministry. Sunday's ministry to God sets the tone for Monday's ministry in the world. And without that, prayer life goes flat.

I know very little about music, but to transpose, I gather, is to put something into another key. And if you don't get in tune with God – if you are out of key with God – the music of the day goes flat. So prayer lifts the workaday world into another sphere, another element. It not only sets the tone of the day, but becomes, hopefully, a sort of background music, against which we live our lives. Whether you are referring to the hour of Sunday's Eucharist or an hour of daily prayer, the prayer is 'transposing in an hour'.

I want to say some brief things about the time of prayer. I was on a television programme some years ago with a woman doctor, an evangelical. She was in a practice with some partners who allowed her enough free time for her plan. She used to have an hour a day for prayer, an afternoon a week, a day a month, and a week a year. Another doctor, Sheila Cassidy, a Roman Catholic, keeps exactly the same plan: an hour a day, an afternoon a week, a day a month, and a week in a year. There's no special virtue in that special plan but I think it's a good one. You must find what rhythm you can.

There is something that Baron Von Hügel said that I think is important. He said, 'Hurry is the death of prayer.' If you've only got five minutes, you have a whole five minutes with God. Any sense of hurry kills prayer.

My next quotation is from François de Sales. He said, 'Every Christian needs an half an hour of prayer each day' – I think he actually needs more than that – 'Each Christian needs an half an hour of prayer each day, except when he is busy, then he needs an hour.' That's absolutely true; he needs it to get out of the sense of hurry.

Remember the people whom I spoke of who do 'transcendental meditation'; they do twenty or thirty minutes twice a day. Remember de Foucauld's direction for the Little Sisters of Jesus which I mentioned, the hour spent in adoration. The novices are taught it is not a time for praying about their family or praying about their sins – that is another activity; this is God's hour. We must give enough time to our prayer.

This note, this tone which is set by prayer, is, Herbert writes, 'a kind of tune which all things hear and fear'. It changes things. It affects the ordinary little things of our lives. If we have this note of prayer, ordinary things will take shape and we will see them in proportion. Things won't get us down or pull us into a dull routine. I don't think routine is quite the same as rhythm. It suggests a plodding with no music in it. You can't transpose routine into the rhythmic tune.

'All things hear and fear' this tune – particularly the devil. The powers of evil fear prayer. They don't want us to pray and they set all manner of difficulties in the way. One difficulty for me has been the desire for sleep. I went to see a very understanding bishop when I had been a Christian for less than a year, and he sent me off to a theological college. After Compline we were supposed to have an hour or two of study in our rooms. I used to open my books and in ten minutes I was sound asleep. I used to flog away at it but one evening I picked up a detective story and found I was wide awake! The devil didn't want me to study. That is how he works. He doesn't urge you to do horrific sins; the chance is that you would be aware of them and repent. The devil hates repentance; it frightens him because it shows that he is loosening his hold on us. He opposes our prayer stealthily because he fears it.

'*Softness, and peace, and joy, and love, and bliss,*
  Exalted manna, gladness of the best,
Heaven in ordinary, man well drest'

Herbert goes on to say that prayer is 'softness, and peace, and joy, and love, and bliss'. Julian of Norwich often used that word 'bliss'. Not all our prayer can be blissful, but there is the banquet side of prayer which has the joy and the love and the peace. As a paradox there is also the other, dark, Gethsemane and Calvary side of prayer. This softness and joy is sometimes given to us by God. People like St Teresa write about the 'consolations' of prayer. God, for encouragement, may give us a consolation, an experience of bliss. When Julian was shown that 'All shall be well and all manner of things shall be well', that was a consolation, a piece of knowledge which God gave to her. We should welcome it when we are given some sweetness or light in prayer, but we ought not to seek them. We are not looking for consolations; we are looking for God. They are not a reward given to those who are specially spiritual; they are gifts to strengthen us, gifts which we need and should save and treasure.

The 'peace and joy' suggest our need to be relaxed. If you go to your prayer with clenched teeth you won't get far. We are not to be frantic in our prayer, even in our intercession. We must be persistent but not frenetic. I think in this respect prayer is rather like learning to drive. You may be tense while you are learning but once you have taken your test and become a good driver you relax. Prayer is a relationship between the lover and the beloved. Sometimes I am the lover and he is the beloved; sometimes he is the lover and I am the beloved. In that relation there can't be tenseness.

Then Herbert says, 'Exalted Manna, gladness of the best.' Exalted manna –

> Bread of heaven, on thee we feed,
> For thy flesh is meat indeed.

Here we are thinking about communion. Communion is only part of what matters in the Eucharist; there is also the 'full, perfect, and sufficient sacrifice, oblation and satisfaction, for the sins of the whole world'. (That's a marvellous bit of grammar; you have to sort it out and find the right adjectives: sufficient sacrifice, perfect oblation, full satisfaction.) But it is the bread which we receive at the Lord's Supper which has the obvious connection with God's feeding of the Israelites with the manna. He gives us food which we digest in prayer. God made provision for his people in the wilderness. They had made golden calves, and they were frightened of the Amalekites and crying to go back to Egypt; and all the time God still cared – as he feeds and cares for us when we are totally rebellious and say we don't want him. He feeds us in our wilderness.

When I first became a practising Christian I wanted to emphasize Christ in me after communion. I learnt then a prayer which I still say every day after receiving communion:

Behold, O Lord Jesu Christ, I now possess thee, who dost possess all things. Wherefore, my God and my all, I beseech thee to withdraw my heart from all things that are not of thee, in which there is naught but vanity and vexation of spirit. On thee alone let my heart be fixed, in thee let my repose be: where my treasure is, there may my heart be also.

The emphasis there is on my possessing Christ. Then, one may hope that, through the years, one grasps the other aspect. One recognizes not only 'he in me' but 'me in him' – the paradox, the other side of the Holy Communion. Remember that Jesus in St John's Gospel says, 'Abide in me and I in you.' William Temple commented, 'Those words, "Abide in me and I in you," contain the whole of Christian spirituality.' Whatever leads to that is good. Whatever hinders it is bad. 'I in you and you in me' is the gist of the spiritual life. The phrase leads to 'enfolded' in him, 'undergirded' by him, 'embraced' by him and all the lovely language of that kind.

And finally: 'Heaven in ordinary, man well drest.' 'Heaven in ordinary' takes us back to the weekday world. That to me means seeing heaven in ordinary things, or being aware of God while we do ordinary things. If our prayer is right and the note is set, we are aware of God even while we speak to people or do our jobs. That constant awareness of God leads us towards adoration.

'A man well drest.' It's not only women who like getting a new hair-do and new clothes; a man also takes pleasure in looking well. 'A man well drest' has a confidence about him. Good clothes give you a boost and put a spring in your steps – and so does prayer.

> 'The milky way, the bird of Paradise,
>   Church-bells beyond the stars heard . . .'

'The milky way' obviously refers to that long cloud of stars, millions of light years across, which we see in the sky at night. If we call prayer the 'Milky Way' the phrase seems to speak of the infinite, immeasurable depths and heights and distances we can travel in prayer. Nowadays we know something about space travel, but we are travellers in eternity which is a different dimension. I find the whole concept fascinating. Of course

Herbert couldn't have known about black holes in space where, friends tell me, the neutron stars have thrown off all their protons and gathered into a mass. When they reach the point of infinity they exert infinite gravity and pull in all the detritus and dust and leave a great black hole. When my mathematical friends start talking about the point of infinity I point out that there is no such thing. It's a conflict in terms. Where is the point of infinity? Where parallel lines meet – nowhere. But it is a concept that is necessary. To me the crucifixion is a great black hole into which God sucks in all the sins of all the ages. They are absorbed and disappear into the infinite gravity of God's love that pulls them and pulls us in towards him.

The Milky Way is all studded with stars. We look up at their blinding beauty on a summer night. But, no matter how many myriads of stars there are, they don't dispel the darkness. John said about Jesus: 'The light shineth in darkness and the darkness overcame it not.' Nor did it overcome the darkness. The light shines in the darkness. In the darkness of depression, of doubt, of despair, or in periods of pain, or in the myriads of kinds of darkness that there are, the light and the darkness coexist. That is what Advent is about. Karl Rahner writes about time being redeemed into eternity. Light and darkness are together here and now. 'Now' is simply eternity in time. Each now is eternity within time. So at the end of every psalm we repeat: 'Glory be to the Father . . . as it was in the beginning, is now and ever shall be.' It sounds best in Latin: 'Sicut erat in principio, et nunc, et semper, et in saecula saeculorum.' 'In the beginning was the word.' Eternity was from the beginning, and ever shall be, and is now.

'Bird of Paradise.' I have never seen one. The dictionary says they are very rare birds with brilliant plumage. The next best thing is a kingfisher, with brilliant colours, beautiful in the sunlight. The kingfisher comes flashing down, but it is elusive and quickly gone. I think it can stand for those quick flashes in our prayer. The gleam is too fast to grasp. You can't catch hold of it, but you can retain the fact that you saw it. It is an affirmation: I know that for a moment I glimpsed eternity. No good your trying to prove to me that I didn't, because I did.

No good my trying to prove to you that I did. It's my own thing that God gave me. 'A bird of Paradise' – a gleam of heaven that flashes across our sight. It can almost blind us.

'Church-bells beyond the stars heard' – a sound from even beyond the Milky Way! They used to speak of the music of the spheres, but this is the music of eternity, the echo of things unheard and undreamt. Somehow they ring bells, deep down within us; they reverberate. 'Church-bells beyond the stars heard' are the music of eternity.

> '. . . the soul's blood,
> The land of spices; something understood.'

'The soul's blood' – I think Herbert shares the Hebrew concept that blood is life. The soul's blood is the soul's life. Prayer is not static; I lean and move towards God, and prayer goes coursing through my veins and my arteries bringing life. If my blood is not functioning properly I get cold. When we are spiritually healthy, prayer is coursing daily through the whole system. We must keep well and beware of hardening of the arteries in the spiritual life. The Psalmist talks about the 'the sickness that destroyeth in the noon-day'. A friend who had his fortieth birthday recently was gloomy to feel he was reaching middle age. Beware of the spirit of middle-age spread! In the old Litany there is a phrase I often use: 'From hardness of heart, and contempt of thy Word and Commandment, Good Lord, deliver us.' This is a word for the depressive who grows so weary with his darkness that he gets a hard heart.

Then prayer is 'the land of spices'. Spices add a little something to give zest to a meal. Prayer adds a spice to things, as a man feels special when he is well dressed. Spices renew your taste when food has seemed distasteful. Cardinal Manning wrote of a lax priest: 'His priesthood ceases to be sweet to him and becomes first tasteless and then bitter in his mouth.' And it isn't only priests for whom religion becomes tasteless and bitter. We are all subject to periods of distaste when the last thing we want to pick up is a spiritual book. This is not so hard to deal with if you treat the period of distaste by sprinkling it with spices from your commonplace book, with bits which you know have meant something to you in the past. Or use a Bible where you have marked verses which struck you. I put purple and red crosses and orange streaks all over the place. If you persevere, the distemper will cure itself. But, in my experience, it is even more important to decide that you are not going to give in. Determine to increase your discipline, your time of prayer and spiritual reading. The devil, who incites the distaste, will back down when he finds that temptation only increases your religion! But he will try something else.

Finally, 'something understood'. The end of prayer is God. Through the life of prayer things become clear. Things begin to come together. Things have more of a meaning and purpose. Young people are always looking for meaning and purpose in life; but if you want purpose you have to look outside life – as the navigator looks up to the pole-star. In prayer, which directs our soul to Almighty God, things begin to come into focus. We begin to understand a little of what God has been doing with us in our life, and with the world. There is much that we cannot understand, as I cannot understand the present suffering of Africa; but I find comfort in Julian: 'I saw truly that nothing is done by hap or by chance but all things by the foreseeing wisdom of God.'

Julian also wrote, 'I saw God in a point.' That momentary awareness is the most common spiritual experience of mankind and the beginning of most people's religion. This seeing God in a point can happen absolutely anywhere – in a church, in a back street in Cambridge, or in any unlikely place. Suddenly, just for a moment, something clicks and things fall into place. Yes, we sense, that's right. This is it. Moses at the burning bush heard God say, 'I am'. Julian knew, 'I it am'. Our experiences may be less explicit and less clearly God, but they are from God and give certainty of God. Most people are given these sudden points, quite often in childhood or at the beginning of their Christian journey.

'Something understood' seems to me to refer to that directly given knowledge and understanding of God. Through our prayer I think God helps us to understand a little of suffering, of evil, and the great questions which we find so difficult. God gives us a little more insight. He allows us to have a little understanding of what he is doing and who he is.

We ought to prepare ourselves to be receptive to what God gives us. We must go to the Bible asking the Spirit to show us what is hidden there for us. That will help us to find a word or a phrase which we can use for a focus, allowing it to resonate within us. Someone has described a simple encounter with God as a colloquy in which God drops a word into your heart, a warm word; and when it cools in your cold heart you throw it back to God to be warmed again. In your prayers, now and again, there will come something which you sense is God's response. It may be a word, or a glimmer of a thought. There is a perception which seems valid even though you cannot express clearly what it is that you perceive. It may not be a bright or happy thing; it may be quite dark. Yet there is a sense of fulfilment and satisfaction, a sense that God is truly there. My experience is that if one has spent almost a whole hour in seeking – and you really do need an hour if that is at all possible – it is often just at the end, out of apparent nothingness, that this answer comes. You may be able to capture God's sign and encapsulate it in a word or a phrase that you can take with you through the day and bring back to your next time of prayer. You have not seen God clearly but you know that something came to you from God. 'Prayer', wrote George Herbert, is 'something understood.'

Part Two

COUNSEL FOR PILGRIMS

Two cities

I journeyed to London, to the timekept City,
There I was told we have too many churches,
And too few chop houses. There I was told
Let the vicars retire. Men do not need the Church
In the place where they work, but where they spend
　　　their Sundays.
In the City we need no bells:
Let them waken the suburbs.

T. S. ELIOT, The Rock

Gonville's pilgrimage brought him to 'the timekept City', to a church with an elegant Wren spire and a rich peal of bells, to a parish where many work but few live. Yet there is always a congregation for the Sunday Eucharist and there are always a few at the daily Communion. And the Eucharist is, he believes, the single most important thing that is done on earth.

Some people come to St Vedast's for its services, for music and glory; others come to pray in its silence; others come to listen and learn. In formal services, with informal groups, and with individuals, Gonville has taught. Most of what follows was recorded by those who heard him at St Vedast's.

Another prayerful priest used to say something like this to those who came to him for counsel. 'I am an old man sitting by the road to Jerusalem. If you like to stop and pass the time of day with me, we can talk about the journey. And I can tell you if you are going in the right direction.' One of the most important things we can do on earth is to set out for heaven, and we are blessed if we know someone who can show us if we are going in the right direction. Here is Gonville talking about that journey and giving practical advice to those who look for a timeless City whose builder and maker is God.

VERA HODGES

4

Starting from where we are

Religion means binding together. It is the search for a link with that source of love and healing which is beyond us. Prayer is the search for a relationship with God.

If we set out to pray we can only start from where we are and, as we are all different, we start from different places. I was born into an atheist family and when I first became a believer, in my middle twenties, it was because I wanted to find some sort of meaning and purpose in life. I started praying to whatever gods there might be; my prayer activity started before my belief in God. I know of others who have started their religion from utter desperation. Others have started through an overplus of joy and wonder, or a feeling that the joy of human love is a reflection of something even greater. It doesn't matter where you start, but somehow you must reach out through your sorrow or your joy, or fear, or anxiety, or whatever possesses you, and try to reach the reality beyond.

Jesus is the greatest teacher about God and about man, so it is sensible to see what he said about prayer. His disciples said to him, 'Lord, teach us to pray.' This was a curious request because they were devout Jews who had been saying their prayers all their lives. Clearly they sensed that Jesus' communication with God was more deep and real than theirs was. Jesus did not just give them a form of words to repeat. He warned them against the pagan idea – still to be found among church people today – that if you say a great many correct words you must be getting somewhere. It is possible to repeat the Lord's Prayer automatically without doing any real praying at all.

Jesus said, 'After this manner therefore pray ye' – that is, in this kind of way. And he started with the word Abba, or Father. The Jews were used to the idea of God as the Father of all life, but Jesus did not use the formal, respectful religious word; he used 'Abba', the familiar family word. So Jesus taught us to begin praying by thinking of God in the way that a small child might turn to his father. Unfortunately some of us can't get much of a picture of fatherhood from our own fathers, but we can all perhaps imagine what we would most wish to be like as parents of our own children. We can picture fatherhood in terms of strength, comfort, belonging and caring – and that is what Abba implies.

Jesus tells us to respond to God by calling him 'Father'. We may speak it in the agonized tone of desperation, or with affection and love and thankfulness. It is the most basic of the words which we may use before God; if we can say it and mean it, then the whole of life takes on a new perspective. Whatever joy or pain or loneliness I may experience, it happens within the fatherhood of God. I know that 'underneath are the everlasting arms', and that I am not a slave but a son. Like the prodigal son, however badly I may behave, I will remain God's son. I belong with Jesus, the son of God. With him I say 'Abba, Father'.

And Jesus also said this: 'When thou prayest, enter into thy closet, and . . . shut the door.' Get alone, get quiet, get away from all the things that attract you or distract you. We cannot develop a relationship with anyone unless we make time to be with that person and speak to him alone. So we need to be alone and face to face with God: human being and Creator, child and Father, Lover and beloved. Alone with God we can begin to build up the relationship of love and trust.

It doesn't matter where you start from. You are God's person. Reach out from where you are and as the person who you are. Be your honest self and don't try to put on any acts or talk to God about what you imagine it is proper to talk to him about. It is you yourself whom he loves and not some false personality which you are trying to put on for his benefit. He may not like you very much as you are, but he loves you and wants you to become something other than you are. This will only begin to happen as you begin to respond to him with the real part of yourself.

When I began to want to be a Christian my first words were, 'If there is a God, this is what I want to say . . .' And I talked of myself and my life and my hopes and fears, and then I tried to talk about him and what I thought he might be and be able to do. It was all very jejune but it was honest. Almost immediately I found I had to get hold of some books on prayer and try to learn to put some order into my response to God.

Many people start with an overflowing sense of thankfulness for human love and friendship, for food and health and strength, for books and letters and all sorts of lovely things. Other people experience a tremendous conviction of sin. They suddenly realize, perhaps through being discovered in some very obvious sin, just how degraded they have become, and so they may well start from penitence. Others have started their prayer because they, or someone they love, has a desperate need for release from pain or terror or some danger which is beyond human control; they may begin with intercession. You can start anywhere, and then you have to work gradually at bringing in the other aspects of prayer which don't come so naturally to you. The great pianist had to begin with five-finger exercises and do a great deal of practising before his magnificent playing began to come naturally to him. You will have to practise the five-finger exercises of prayer before all sides of it are natural to you. Sometimes adoration will not come for a long, long time, so I think it is a good thing to practise it by using other people's words. Books like E. Milner-White's *My God, My Glory* may help, and there are the Psalms which proclaim the glory of God. It is not hypocritical to use other people's words even when we cannot mean them whole-heartedly; it is part of learning and growing.

If you are honestly trying to stretch out towards God, you may be surprised to find how soon you are beginning to love him. Yet it is not surprising, because it is only human to love what is worthwhile when we begin to know its value. We begin to love God when we want to love him and see that we exist to love him and to be loved by him.

This love and knowledge cannot grow without disciplined effort on our part, but this is where many people's religion breaks down. They go to church and try to be kindly to their neighbours but they make no disciplined attempt to know God in any real sense. Then loving him seems impossible, and ultimately serving him becomes impossible too.

If you want to make progress in the Christian life it is essential to carve some specific time out of your life for this activity. I should say that the very barest possible minimum is a quarter of an hour in a day, but if you can really manage only three minutes, try to find some time once a week when you can give a longer period. One period of half an hour is better than two periods of fifteen minutes, because the longer you get to soak yourself in prayer, to slough off the world and attempt to be with God, the better it is. Ideally, the early morning is the best time for this. If you make your main prayer at night you will probably be too tired and too full of the events of the day to be fully capable of responding whole-heartedly to God. I find kneeling beside my bed at night is much too conducive to going to sleep there and then. But individuals must work out the programme which fits them; they may be able to pray in the lunch hour, or when the baby is asleep.

Some people get worried about the right posture for prayer. The most natural position for most Western people does seem to be on their knees, although in recent years I have found it easier to pray sitting down. I have sometimes found it valuable to pray standing up with arms outstretched. The kind of posture does not really matter at all provided that it is a position in which you can pray, and that should mean a position in which you are fairly relaxed and yet likely to keep alert.

Writers on prayer say that the way to begin is by recollection. This simply means that you have been dissipated – that is, fragmented – by your response to all sorts of people and things and you need to collect yourself together into one person, into yourself, so that the whole of yourself can begin to turn towards God and respond to him. Some people do this recollection by reading a passage from the Bible. Others look at a crucifix or a picture or repeat a particular phrase, and I would advise you

to experiment with all these methods. My own personal habit
is taken from the Eastern mystics. I find it very valuable to
take about ten deep breaths. I think of the way the Spirit of
God moved over the face of the waters at the creation, and
brought cosmos out of chaos; I think of the wind of Pentecost
and ask that the breath of God may enter into my being and
calm and collect me.

Often, as soon as I start to pray all sorts of other things come
into my mind. I ought to try to discard some of them at once,
but some are valuable ideas, like the need to remember to buy
sausages, or the fact that I ought to write to Mrs So-and-So.
It's useful to have paper and pencil handy to make a note of
these things. I find this less distracting than saying to myself,
'I mustn't be thinking about sausages when I am saying my
prayers.' It gets the sausages out of the way and the prayer
goes more easily. I may have good ideas about God or about
prayer itself and I can write those down too. You may be able
to incorporate your wandering thoughts into your prayers. If
you think of Mrs So-and-So you can bring her into your prayer.
If you think of something good which has happened, then thank
God for it; if you think of something bad, think of it with
sorrow and ask for healing. If you have a concern for the
future, bring it into your prayer for God's blessing. Above all
don't be angry with yourself when different thoughts come in
but move through them to find God.

As you read about prayer you will find that writers often
divide it into three stages. There is vocal prayer in which we
do a lot of talking. There is mental prayer in which we do the
listening. There is contemplative prayer in which there do not
seem to be many words on either side but just a joy in
communication. My own experience is that prayer, rather than
being a sort of ladder up which one progresses laboriously
through these different stages, is much more like a spiral in
which one comes back and back again to the same point but
each time at a rather higher (or deeper) level than the time
before. You will need to try out the different approaches for
yourself.

You will want to learn how to make a conscious effort to

listen to what God has to say to you. Many people begin to practise mental prayer through some sort of meditation. Often they begin this by reading a short passage from the Bible and considering what, through these words, Jesus is saying to them in their own particular situation. It is a good thing to use our imagination to build up a clear picture of Jesus saying these words, or of something which these words suggest to us. This use of our imagination helps us to listen and not let our minds wander. Some people find that they can listen to God best by looking at a picture or through listening to music.

Some people find that thoughtful, imaginative, meditation seems a fussy approach to prayer. The word 'colloquy' is used sometimes for a simpler way of prayer in which we speak a word or two to God and he returns it with a deeper meaning. Often we want to repeat words over and over, just as we do in human love. We may repeat the name of Jesus or some phrase from the Gospels, like 'My God and my all'. Jesus said, 'Seek, and ye shall find; knock and it shall be opened unto you.' So we knock and wait – but gently, not banging desperately or anxiously at the door. It may well be that we will soon be given some experience of contemplative prayer in which we are satisfied though no word is uttered. We will come back to this later. The main thing is just to start praying. Close your door, quieten yourself, and long for God – even if your longing does not amount to very much.

5

Growing in relationship

Our prayer is a search for a relationship with God. Writers have described the growth of this relationship. They say that if we could suddenly see God revealed in all his glory, our response would be one of awestruck wonder. Picture the breathless, speechless wonder of a small child who is taken into a darkened room at Christmas and shown the Christmas lights burning on the tree. If I could see God, those writers say, my response would be wonder and adoration. The next feeling that would come to me would be one of horror at myself when I compare myself with the great glory of love sweeping down towards me, so my second reaction would be sorrow and contrition. Then, ideally, I would realize that God still loved me in spite of the awful things I had done, so I would go on to thanksgiving. Finally, I would go on to supplication, to plead for God's help for me and for those I love. So I would begin to pray those four main kinds of prayer: adoration, contrition, thanksgiving and supplication.

But I do not think that it happens just like that for most of us. We are too blind to see God in all his glory. We see the divine glory reflected in earthly things; we see it piecemeal and in different ways. An engineer or a mathematician may have an idea of loveliness which is quite different from that of a gardener or a farmer. A young lover, perhaps, will conceive of glorious beauty through his experience of his girl's body and the joy of their relationship together. These things may suggest little corners of God's glory.

As God draws us, and as we feel our way, we will develop these main aspects of prayer: adoration, contrition, thanksgiving, and supplication. Aspects of adoration and supplication have been given chapters to themselves, but first I want to say a little about thanksgiving and contrition, and about praise – which is part of adoration – and about the place of complaint in our prayers.

Contrition and thanksgiving go naturally together because almost everything that happens to us should be the subject of one or the other. First, let us take a look at contrition. Little boys caught stealing apples may be sorry, but they are probably sorry just about being caught, in which case they feel remorse, not contrition. Remorse does not do anyone any good. Contrition on the other hand is the realization that something one has done is wrong and that one is really sorry that one has done it.

We have all sometimes deliberately done wrong. We have forfeited our status as children of God by turning away; we have left home like the prodigal son, taking the gifts of God with us. At such times, we are like the man found guilty in law who has no right to claim anything but submits himself to the mercy of the court and asks for clemency; or like the man who can't pay his rent and can only ask for his landlord's mercy. When we are in debt to God – when, as the confession in the Prayerbook puts it, 'the burden of our sins is intolerable' – all we can do is to throw ourselves on the mercy of God, asking that his mercy will cover us, cloak us, encompass us, lest we get what we deserve.

The two Hebrew words for mercy are helpful in illustrating this aspect of God's love. One of these words means 'to be motherly', and this may help some people who have a hang-up about the so-called masculinity of God. When we think of God as our Father there is certainly a danger of getting tangled up with the stereotype of a demanding father, wanting the best from his son and expecting a high standard of conduct. However, it is less typical of a mother to care in this kind of way; she cares for us in spite of our conduct, embracing us and holding us in love even though we are not good sons or daughters. The other word has the meaning 'to bend down', which evokes the picture of a mother bending over a child in her arms. A psychiatrist will tell you that one of the most important features of a child's development is the confidence given by the love shining in the mother's face. So when we turn in contrition to God's mercy, we can have confidence in this mother aspect of God bending down over us.

Why give thanks to God? Certainly not because he wants to be thanked, like an aunt who has given a Christmas present. Thanksgiving springs out of a basic gut realization that we are totally dependent on God for everything. We have nothing of our own, and by thanking God constantly we are able to drive this knowledge deeper and deeper into ourselves so that we develop a continual awareness of the goodness and givenness of things. If we do not give thanks for them it is easy to take God's gifts for granted, gifts like personality, background, upbringing, freedom from fear, freedom from pain (think how marvellous it is to have a whole day free from pain), and gifts like appetite, sight, hearing – everything. These are tremendous gifts and we need to express our realization of them in thanksgiving. If you can't think of anything to thank God for, you will get some idea by simply reading through a dictionary! And the ability to read, whether words or music, is another cause for thanksgiving. Everything we see and feel and experience has a value and represents our total dependence on God.

The best way I have found to express contrition on the one hand and thanksgiving on the other is to sit down at the end of the day: and, despite what I said earlier, this particular kind of prayer is best done at night, but preferably sitting rather than kneeling by your bed. Just examine the past day. 'I got up this morning – thank God for my sleep and safety through the dark hours. But I didn't get up early enough to say my prayers properly – I'm very sorry about that; I've got to watch it. I ought to use my alarm clock. Then I had breakfast, and I thank God for that; but it's a long time since I gave any money to Christian Aid for feeding other people. And I grumbled that the coffee was cold. Then I took the bus to work and that was lovely because I caught one and it got there on time.' Or alternatively – 'I had to wait ages and got angry although there was nothing I could do about it. I arrived at the office – thank

God I have a job . . .' Try to look back through each incident of the day. You will be surprised how much of the day has just slid away; it is a pity that we forget so easily, but if you keep on practising this process of recall, things will start coming back more clearly.

You may find that your memory of some incidents brings real pain or sorrow, and then your prayer will become petition or intercession or complaint. Most memories will be a matter either for contrition or thanksgiving. For instance, if I am lucky enough to have two whiskies before dinner I will thank God for them. If I am stupid enough, and rich enough, to have seven whiskies before dinner, I should have to be sorry about it! Incidentally, in this kind of prayer it is particularly important to follow one of my earlier suggestions and have paper and pencil with you, so that as you go through the day you can write down the omissions, letters you ought to have written, things you ought to have said, and so on. Unless they are written down you will forget them again and they will not get done.

Praising and complaining, again, are two kinds of prayer which are essentially complementary to each other. First, praise – and let it be clear that praise is radically different from thanksgiving. When we give thanks we are focusing on what God does for us, whereas praise is simply appreciating God for what he is. Let us also be clear that praise is not designed to stop God being angry – like patting that intimidating dog. God does not need praise and certainly does not need to be told how good he is. Praise expresses our need, not his. The real 'I' within me is athirst for God. We have a deep longing for God, not just for his gifts, his peace, his strength, or anything else, but for God himself. So we need to stretch out to the Lord God, to try to love him, to try to put into words some recognition of his glory, his wonder and his love.

Praise needs only a few words. It is not the quantity of words but the quality of their reach which matters. If you cannot find the words yourself, try using the opening to the 'Te Deum' from the Book of Common Prayer.

We praise thee, O God:
we acknowledge thee to be the Lord.
All the earth doth worship thee:
the Father everlasting.

There will probably be an undercurrent of protest in your mind
that it is not true, that 'all the earth' does not worship him –
in fact you don't really worship him yourself. But just a bit of
you would like it to be true, and would like to join in with the
Angels crying aloud with 'the Heavens and all the Powers
therein,' to merge your own voice in that great cosmic shout
of praise: 'Holy, Holy, Holy . . .' The 'Te Deum' is marvellous, but there are many other hymns and psalms and canticles
whose words may help to light up the praise in your own
heart.

The need to complain is an important complement to the
prayer of praise. Most of us suffer at some time or other in our
lives. We may suffer pain or depression or injustice or betrayal
by our friends, or the loss of love, or the agony of watching
someone we love dying inexorably of an incurable disease. If
that sort of thing happens, it is no good denying your feelings
and smiling politely and saying you are sure it is all for the best
and there will be pie-in-the-sky when we die. If you honestly
feel that there is something radically wrong and don't express
it, then you are not being yourself, and it is yourself whom
God loves. No mother would want a badly hurt child to pretend
that it is not in pain. You are a child of God and you owe it
to yourself and to him, your Father, to be yourself and openly
to express to him what you are going through and what you
feel about it. Complaining to other people may bring rejections;
they may have enough troubles of their own, or may not be
able to take it. But we have solid evidence that God can take
it. This is precisely what happened on the cross. Men rejected
him, spat at him, betrayed him, hit him in the face, flogged
him, and he went on loving them. So there is nothing that you
can do or say to God that will stop him loving you. Curse God
if you must; he will not reject you. Certainly complain to him,
perhaps using Our Lord's great prayer of complaint, 'My God,

my God, why have you forsaken me?' If Our Lord said it, you can.

Use the psalms which are full of prayers of complaint. 'Why art thou so heavy, O my soul, and why art thou so disquieted within me?' – that fits when you are caught in depression and there seems no way out. Or 'Why do the ungodly come on so fast?' – when everyone else seems to be having a marvellous time, and you, who are a Christian, are left out in the cold. These are genuine prayers which reflect reality. If all you can pray is complaint, that's fine; you have been yourself and related your predicament to God, and that is real prayer. If you can add some words like, 'I hate what is happening but help me to try to make use of it, or grow through it', this will help. If you can't say that sincerely, then don't say it.

6

Praying with others

We have spoken of the prayer of the person who enters into his closet and closes the door. This suggests that Christian prayer is a private business, but nothing could be further from the truth. The people of God learn to pray together both in small groups, in churches, and in spiritual community with the whole company of heaven.

Jesus chose twelve disciples. We may find that Christian love and trust can be developed best in small groups, say of seven or eight. A group may meet for prayer or study. Perhaps they are neighbours, or work at the same job, or the group may be an offshoot of a larger congregation. Membership of such a group strengthens a Christian's faith; perhaps it is the one thing which enables him to keep going. And infection works for good as well as for bad; if Christian love and trust and healing begin to flow in a small group, they are bound to flow outwards to the wider congregation and to the wider world.

I used to be Warden of a non-denominational movement, the Servants of Christ the King, whose members are committed to learning to pray, talk, and work together. The dynamic of this movement lies in the process which we call 'waiting upon God'. This means for us a half-hour's silence, followed by controlled discussion, by open discussion, and finally by decision for action. The phrase 'waiting upon God' may sound rather passive, but I don't know a better one. The best hotel-waiters are willing and attentive, and our 'waiting' should be expectant and attentive too. A leader may read a passage from the Bible, and then we pray in silence. Then everyone in turn tells the others what has come to his mind during the silence;

this is what we mean by controlled discussion. After that follows open discussion which generally shows up some common concern and the way in which we can meet it. We may end by taking each other's hands and saying the grace together.

This kind of prayer teaches and deepens our Christian fellowship. It is by our ability to make good human relationships that Christians should be distinguished – 'By this shall all men know that ye are my disciples, if ye have love one to another.' 'One to another' is, strictly speaking, a one-to-one relationship; though this should develop into a group relationship. We are learning to love 'as I have loved you', as Christ loved his companions.

Now Christ demonstrated his love for his disciples in two ways. First he washed their feet, then he died for them. The story of the foot-washing (John 13) points to qualities which ought to be shown in our own love for each other. Christ's action seems to have been spontaneous; during the supper he rose, 'laid aside his garments, and took a towel and girded himself,' acting in response to what he felt in his heart. The disciples were desolate, if not desperate; it seemed to them that Jesus was leaving them and they were told 'where I go ye cannot come'. They had given up everything to follow him and now he was leaving them – it was all very well his talking about sending them 'another Comforter', but it was him that they had learnt to trust, and him alone they wanted. They needed comfort, comfort deeper than words could convey. Our Lord had been comforted himself by the woman who had washed his own feet and dried them with her hair (John 12:3 and Matt. 26:6–13), so he was moved to do something of the sort for them so that they might be comforted too. With strong, gentle, healing hands he handled, almost fondled, each foot in turn, that each one of the Twelve might feel his love flowing through.

So our Christian love should arise out of the heart, in response to the needs of others. The need may be unspoken and the response, like Our Lord's, may well be unspoken also. Words can sometimes damage relationships which are beginning to grow. Language, beautiful, precise, complex as it is, is still a most inadequate means of communication. It is in silence of the kind that I am describing that we may regain our largely lost powers of telepathy and grow towards each other in love and understanding. And this understanding may be promoted by little acts of mutual service.

Behind the actions lie the attitudes. 'See that ye love each other with a pure heart fervently,' says St Peter. Which is what we don't really want! We much prefer St Paul's 'Be kindly affectioned one to another with brotherly love'. That's much more our cup of tea. We don't mind, we even like, a warm relationship, but 'fervently' is a bit much. It means 'hot', 'glowing', 'ardent', 'intense', and we are inclined to dread this kind of relationship. We don't really want to get too deeply involved with each other – but that is the quality of love that is demanded of us. I believe that if we could get over this hump of resistance within ourselves to reach real love, then we could begin to make the unique contributions that Christians could make in the whole sphere of human relationship – at all levels and throughout the world.

Then, as we pray together as a group, how can we learn to love each other and to commit ourselves to each other as well as to Christ? I think we should make a silent act of reconciliation, reaching out towards each member of the group in turn. When I first started to practise this I imagined myself kneeling in front of each member of the group in turn and asking for two things. First I asked, as I still ask, for forgiveness – forgiveness for any way in which I might have hurt them consciously or unconsciously; and for things of which they may be totally unaware, such as a judgement or hasty criticism made behind their backs or even interiorly in my own mind. Then I imagined myself asking for acceptance – that they would accept me with my faults: those habits of mine which may, quite unknown to me, irk or annoy another; my obvious failure to love others as I ought, and so on.

Then I imagined myself standing in front of each one, as it were, and offering any forgiveness they may want, or need, of me; accepting each as he or she is, with those things about them that I find difficult or tiresome; embracing each one, which means not only putting my arms around them (in imagination) but bracing or strengthening them and enfolding them, surrounding them with love. In this acceptance of others I would dwell as little as I could upon their faults and prickles and as much as possible on him or her, the person himself or herself, hiding behind the facade that we all present towards each other. So I go round the group, each one individually in turn, praying as deeply as I can, praying with them and for them, for their needs at all levels as far as I can discern them; then for each one and me together, that we may grow closer to each other in understanding and love.

Another variation of this practice is to go round the group and consider each person's burdens. St Paul wrote, 'Bear ye one another's burdens and so fulfil the law of Christ.' And the law of Christ is 'that ye love one another as I have loved you'. We all have burdens: some of them are 'grievous to be borne' and some are burdens willingly undertaken; they can all be shared, and each person is lightened by that sharing. So I think round the group and consider each person's burdens. One may have a heavy work-load or a job which he does not enjoy or find fulfilling. Another may bear the burden of ill-health or old age, or growing deafness. Some have worries or fears – and anxieties are just as real a burden if they are about largely imaginary ills. Others are burdened by their own natures, by an inability to make relationships, to love and to be loved. For another the burden is loneliness. As I imagine each person's burden I try, in imagination, to put my shoulder under that burden with him or her, to feel the weight and take some of it on myself. I believe that the power of love and prayer draws us closer and enables us to share each other's loads. And, as I try to lift something for others, I put my own burdens, silently, into the pool of the group's presence, knowing that others are willing to share their weight with me and so soften their hurt. We have all been hurt, wounded by our own sins, by the sins of others, by the limitations of our upbringing; but we can help to heal each other and make way for God's healing to flow.

Another approach which helps us to grow in mutual love has been described as 'passing autobiographically into others' lives and then coming back enriched to one's own standpoint and to a new understanding of one's own life' (John Dunne in *The Way of all the Earth* and *Search for God in Time and Memory*). This means considering what we know of a person's life and trying to empathize with his experiences, sensing his tastes, his enjoyments, his joys and sorrows, his glories and his glooms.

We hear glib talk of breaking down the barriers of class, colour, creed or whatever. There are many barriers to love inside each of us. We resist invasion; we refuse to face the truth about ourselves; we raise walls of pride and shame. We can only let the barriers down very gently, by silently sharing things which we dare not show. Perhaps in time we may be able to verbalize some little bit of it, or to communicate it by a touch or a look – which is enough: the rest can be left unsaid.

If we are able to practise this mutual identification with each other with any reality we shall be getting as close to the heart of Christian love as we can really get. It is something deeper than a relationship between an 'I' here and a 'thou' there: it is a coming together in which, in some sense, we become one. This is the kind of love revealed in the incarnation: the Son of God 'was made man', totally identified with us by his birth and death. And it was what Jesus was on about in his prayer at the Last Supper when he prayed 'that they all may be one: as Thou, Father, art in me and I in Thee, that they also may one in us . . . I in them and Thou in me that they may be made perfect in one'. I do not believe this to be possible for human beings except in Christ.

At the Last Supper Christ washed his disciples' feet; and afterwards he died for them. Generally, at the present time, this kind of love is not demanded of us, though there are parts of the world where it can mean death for people to call themselves Christian. We would do well to consider whether, if occasion were to rise, we would be willing to die for each other. I doubt whether many of us would be willing in cold blood to pledge ourselves to do so; but I have an idea that in the last resort we might – just – rise to it, if we try to practise real love 'in Christ' before the time comes.

When we pray together, we grow. 'When two or three are gathered together there am I in the midst of them' (Matt.

18:20). That is not only the teaching of Christ, it is also a fact of experience.

7

Praying with the Church

The experience of praying with a small group may help us to share the life of the Church; but it is through the Eucharist that we are likely to become most aware of the Church in its widest sense, of the whole body of Christ, the whole household of God, the whole communion of saints. All Christians are saints – however hypocritical or neurotic or just plain bad we may be – because we know that we are loved and redeemed and made holy for the service of love. Jesus told us that the distinguishing mark of his disciples is their love for each other. We cannot love by ourselves. We are bound together and belong together in the 'fellowship of the Holy Spirit'.

I myself did not begin to realize the depth and width and gloriousness of the fellowship of the Spirit until I found myself cut off from all natural human contact in the prison cells of the South African Security Police. I stood each morning facing the two windows of my cell and I imagined a great crucifix hanging in front of me. And there I went through what I could remember of the words of the Mass. When the time came to do the actual things which Jesus taught us to do, in remembrance of him, I had no bread or wine to offer. But as I imagined myself taking these two common gifts I said the words which Jesus taught us to say: 'This is my body, this is my blood,' and the mysteries became alive. 'Therefore with angels and archangels and all the whole company of heaven' – I don't think I've ever known the reality of the company of heaven as I did in that prison cell. Neither had I ever before even known what the Church was. As an Anglo-Catholic I used to have rather a narrow view of the Church. Now I know the Church is 'the company of the beloved', whether they are Quakers, or Romans, or – what does it matter? When it came to the time of the consecration I took – I didn't have any bread and wine – I took nothing into my hands and I said, 'This is my body, which is given for you. Do this in remembrance of me.' And again I took nothing into my hands and I said, 'This is the blood of the New Testament, which is shed for you and for many, for the remission of sins. Do this as often as you shall drink it in remembrance of me.' The Communions which I received in that prison cell, in that way, without the means of bread and wine, were as real and as glorious and as triumphant and as magnificent as any Communion I have ever received in my own cathedral, with the organ going and the incense and the bells and all the glory. They were just as real and wholly as healing and as complete. That is my witness.

The great central act of worship observed by almost all the Christian churches is known by many names: the Holy Communion, the Eucharist, the Lord's Supper, the Breaking of Bread, the Liturgy, and the Mass. It does not matter what you call it. More and more Christian churches are making it the centre and focus of their worship.

The Eucharist is celebrated for many reasons, and primarily because Our Lord commands us to do it and to continue to do it 'until his coming again'. 'Was ever another commandment so obeyed?' asks Gregory Dix:

For century after century, spreading slowly to every continent and country and among every race on earth, this action has been done, in every conceivable human need from infancy and before it to extreme old age and after it, from the pinnacles of earthly greatness to the refuge of fugitives in the caves and dens of the earth. Men have found no better thing than this to do for kings at their crowning and for criminals going to the scaffold; for armies in triumph or for a bride and bridegroom in a little country church; for the proclamation of a dogma or for a good crop of wheat; for the wisdom of the Parliament of a mighty nation or for a sick old woman afraid to die; for a schoolboy sitting an examination or for Columbus setting out to discover America; for the famine of whole provinces or for the soul of a dead lover; in thankfulness because my father did not die of pneumonia; for a village headman much tempted to return to fetich because the yams had failed; because the Turk was at the gates of Vienna; for the repentance of Margaret; for the settlement of a strike; for a son for a barren woman; for Captain so and so, wounded and prisoner of war; while lions roared in the nearby amphitheatre; on the beach at Dunkirk; while the hiss of scythes in the thick June grass came faintly through the windows of the church; tremulously, by an old monk on the fiftieth anniversary of his vows; furtively by an exiled bishop who had hewn timber all day in a prison camp near Murmansk; gorgeously, for the canonisation of S. Joan of Arc – one could fill many pages with the reasons why men have done this and not tell a hundredth part of them. And best of all, week by week, and month by month on a hundred thousand successive Sundays, faithfully, unfailingly, across the parishes of christendom, the pastors have done just this . . .

(The Shape of the Liturgy)

And most of you will seek Communion, not in a prison cell, nor in Johannesburg Cathedral, nor at my church of St Vedast's, but at one of the thousands of parish churches where, 'faithfully, unfailingly', the Eucharist is celebrated. Some of you will hear the words from the 1662 Book of Common Prayer, while more of you perhaps will hear the words of Rite A or Rite B from the 1980 Alternative Service Book. You may join a small house-group celebrating the holy mysteries round a kitchen table where you trust and know the people there and feel that they are a true community. You may attend an 8 o'clock service with two or three old ladies. You may attend a friendly parish communion. You may go to some glorious High Mass with a sense of mystery and wonder conveyed by music, incense, bells, and whatever adjuncts may be helpful in lifting us out of the ordinary world. What matters is that you should be able to sense the glory, and the awefulness of Christ's sacrifice, and the sense that we are reaching up to God and he is coming down to us.

I want to lead you through the service looking at what it is and what it does. One of the ways in which it can be looked at is as a journey in which you and I are going to meet our Lord. Different rites vary the order a little and differ here and there, so I just point out some of the main features.

The journey begins when the priest comes in. Generally he is wearing traditional vestments which have meaning and significance. Their colour may mark the season; as white for great feasts like Christmas and Easter; red to symbolize blood or fire, for feasts of martyrs and of the Holy Spirit; purple for Advent and Lent; green for ordinary days. Sometimes the altar is censed at the beginning of the service and the use of incense marks other important points through the service. This reminds us of the burnt offerings of the Old Testament which were superseded by Christ's perfect sacrifice on the cross. As the dry gum of the incense is put on the burning charcoal smoke rises and can remind us that when we are put in touch with the Lord Christ he and we together can make something happen in the world. The smoke as it rises and spreads reminds us that our own prayers flow together with the prayer of the Church triumphant, with the prayers of the saints which, it is said in Revelation, 'are as incense rising'.

We may begin with a hymn or an introit which sets the tone of the day. Before we set out we say the Collect for Purity because we need purity if we are going to meet Our Lord in his glory. We are in sin and we ask the Father, the Son, and the Spirit in turn to 'have mercy'. Then we look towards the mountain peak, the goal of our journey. We sing or say the 'Gloria' which is a great shout of praise and confidence in the glory and mercy and holiness of the God towards whom we journey.

The next part of the service is for listening and learning. We say the Collect which is proper, or special for that particular day. We sit to hear the Epistle which is part of a letter, a sort of family letter, written by a Christian to his fellow Christians. Then we get ready for the Gospel. The Greek for gospel is *euangelion* – a lovely word that goes 'clang' or 'bang', and that is the way the Gospel should be; it is meant to make a bang in the world. In the Gospel we hear our Lord's words for the first time in the service, or else something is said about him. We treat this first peak in our journey with some ceremony, at the least we stand to listen, like soldiers awaiting orders.

After the Gospel comes the sermon. This is normally an explanation of the Gospel and how it applies to modern life. It is important to remember that a sermon is a two-way thing – if it is just a priest talking while the congregation goes to sleep, it is not going to get anyone anywhere. Both priest and people should have been praying that they may get some crumbs of thought from it. If the preacher seems to have been talking eyewash, or if he has been stimulating or helpful, it is useful to tell him. How else can he learn what needs to be said?

The sermon is followed by the Creed which proclaims our faith. In it we proclaim our belief in God's love, shown to us by Christ, who is

> God of God, Light of Light, Very God of very God, Begotten, not made, Being of one substance with the Father, By whom all things were made: Who for us men, and for our salvation came down from heaven, And was incarnate by the Holy Ghost of the Virgin Mary, And was made man . . .

Composers seldom treat it this way but the Creed should be a tremendous song of triumph: this is what we hold; martyrs have died for it and it is our faith for ever.

Now we pray for the Church and the world. In the Book of Common Prayer we pray for 'the whole state of Christ's Church' in words which reflect our Lord's prayer at the Last Supper (John 17) when he prayed first for his disciples and then for 'those also which shall believe on me through their word'. The main burden of Jesus' high priestly prayer is prayer for unity: not in the first instance for church unity but for union, unity, with him, with the Father, Son and Spirit, 'that they may be one in us, I in them and they in me'. We pray for unity with God, for the unity we are going to receive in Holy Communion.

And we pray for union with each other, asking 'to all thy people give thy heavenly grace and specially to this congregation here present'. When I was training I was taught that I should be quiet for a moment or two at this point while I prayed with and for the congregation and they prayed for each other. The newer rites make an opportunity for members of the congregation to lead the intercession and to pray about topical events or affairs of the local church. Whichever form we use this is a point for offering to God the nations of the world, the sick and the suffering, all that we want God to bless, all whom we love and all who are engaged with us on the pilgrimage to God, and the faithful departed who have completed their journey. We remember our own departed who are close to us and the saints in glory who are one with us.

We have come a long way towards the point where we meet Christ in the Communion. To prepare for the final assault on the peak of the mountain, like mountaineers of other kinds, we need to get rid of any weight and clutter which holds us back. We rid ourselves of the weight of our sins by making our confession together. We acknowledge that we have sinned against God and each other and we receive the priest's absolution.

We go on to acknowledge our unworthiness to share in the Communion. The Prayer of Humble Access, which begins 'We do not presume to come to this thy table', is a very lovely and peculiarly Anglican prayer. Its theme is God, 'whose property [or nature] is always to have mercy'. It sets out the Anglican doctrine of the meaning of Holy Communion in words which echo the prayerbook catechism. There the question is asked, 'What is the inward part or thing signified in the Lord's Supper?', and the answer is, 'The Body and Blood of Christ which are verily and indeed taken and received by the faithful in the Lord's Supper.' In the prayer we ask that God may grant us 'so to eat the flesh of your dear son Jesus Christ and to drink his blood . . .' Jesus said, 'I am the living bread' – the bread that is alive. It has the power of the body of Christ within it, and the wine contains his splendid risen life. I do not understand it, but I have experienced it and I believe it.

In modern services the rite is built clearly round the four actions of Jesus at the Last Supper: he took, he blessed, he broke and he gave. Before the priest can take the bread and wine and bless it, it must be brought to the altar. Our 'alms' (the collection) and 'oblations' (the bread and wine) are brought up by lay people, or taken from a side table. Before this, or sometimes rather later, many churches observe 'the peace'. In early days of the Church, Christians gave each other a kiss of peace and now, when the priest says, 'The peace of the Lord be always with you,' the people may greet each other by taking each other's hands, or in some other way.

We begin our assault on the peak. The priest will turn and say, 'The Lord be with you,' which really means, 'Are you OK? Are you with me?' and our reply means, 'You bet we are.' And then 'Lift up your hearts.' 'We lift them up unto the Lord.' And so the climb is on. We go on and on, up and up, until we come to the great song which Isaiah heard in his vision of heaven: 'Holy, Holy, Holy, Lord God of Hosts. Heaven and earth are full of thy glory. Glory be to thee, O Lord most high.' We are almost at the top, joining in worship with the whole of redeemed creation.

We reach up, but we cannot reach right up to the Holy of Holies where God is. We can go no higher, but Christ can come down to us, as he did at the incarnation. 'Blessed is he who cometh in the name of the Lord.'

The prayer of consecration reminds us of the Last Supper, but it begins not with that but with the death of Christ, when (ASB, Rite A) 'He opened wide his arms for us on the cross' and (BCP) 'made a full, perfect and sufficient sacrifice for the sins of the whole world'. Endless books have been written about what those words mean. Here we are concerned that it happened and that we are commanded as Christians 'to continue' a remembrance 'of that his precious death'. That is a remembrance, not in the sense of looking back into the past, but in a special sense of bringing the significance of Christ's passion and death into the present and into our lives. Now Christ is with us and we reach out to adore. We may use the Lord's Prayer here.

The priest takes a wafer of bread – which has become the Body of Christ – and breaks it, as Christ broke the bread at the Last Supper. You may hear the 'fraction', which represents the crucifixion. After this we often address the ascended Christ directly in the anthem, 'O Lamb of God that takest away the sins of the world, have mercy upon us'. But remember that this is not a little baa-lamb; he is the lamb who is also called the Lion of Judah. He is the symbol of sacrifice, as St John the Divine describes him in Revelation. He is Christ who 'ever liveth to make intercession for us', pleading the sacrifice which broke down the barriers between God and man. And we, in the 'Agnus Dei', join with the risen Christ to plead his sacrifice for ourselves and all our brothers in the world.

Now the journey is complete. The priest receives the Holy Communion himself and we come up to the altar and it is given to us. We may say to ourselves: 'Lord, I am not worthy that thou shouldst come under my roof, but speak the word only, and my soul shall be healed.' The old prayer-book words for administering communion are: 'The body of our Lord Jesus Christ . . . preserve thy body and soul . . .' Remember that there is healing for the body as well as the soul. And remember that this is never 'my communion': it is 'our communion', for when we receive Christ we receive him with each other. We in his Church are members of one another who need each other and belong together. That is what *koinonia* 'the fellowship of the Holy Spirit' is all about.

We say a final prayer of thanksgiving together, and a blessing follows in which we are told that the 'peace of God which passeth all understanding' will keep our hearts and minds. This is peace under the rule of the victor who has broken the chains of death and hell – may that peace grow in your hearts and be around you in your home and your work, and throughout this country and throughout the nations of the world. And we are dismissed: 'Go in peace to love and serve the Lord.'

There may be coffee afterwards, or a glass of wine in the church hall, or other opportunity to get to know our fellow Christians. But first we must remember to say our own personal thank you. We have come through our journey; we have been enriched and strengthened by it ourselves and given something to the community through our participation. We have prayed with the Church which, in giving us the sacrament, has given us a tangible link with the work of Christ and a lifeline between heaven and earth.

8

The way of sacrifice

We have looked at the Eucharist as a journey leading to our own communion. But there is a great deal more to the service than its just being a kind of machinery by which Holy Communion is produced. We will deepen our understanding of the mighty acts in which we share, if we look at Christ's own part in the Mass. And I prefer to use the word 'Mass' here, because it does not stress a special aspect of the service, as Holy Communion or Eucharist (meaning thanksgiving) relate to our own part in the action; Mass, with its less limited reference, is appropriate when we look at the whole meaning of the whole eucharistic action which is more than the reception of the body and blood of our glorified Saviour.

The prayer-book catechism asks, 'Why was the sacrament of the Lord's Supper ordained?' and gives the answer, 'for the continual remembrance of the sacrifice of the death of Christ and of the benefits which we receive thereby'. The Mass is in some way a microcosm of what Christ does upon the cross. He said of himself, 'As Moses lifted up the serpent in the wilderness even so must the Son of Man be lifted up.' In these words he 'signified the death by which he should die'. He was lifted up on the cross and we can see a further meaning there: he is in some way lifted up to God the Father for us each time we celebrate the Mass.

> Having with us him who pleads above,
> We here present, we here set forth to thee
> That only offering perfect in thine eyes,
> The one pure true and only sacrifice.

In our prayer we are looking to Jesus as the lamb sacrificed for us. To understand that we must look back to the Bible. The Israelites would choose a lamb and set it apart for God. The lamb was killed, that's to say, its life was taken, and that life, in the shape of blood, was offered to God. There were several ideas behind this. It was an acknowledgement of God's right to share in his own creation. Compare this with the words: 'All things come from you, and of your own do we give you' (ASB). Then there was the idea that giving a sacrifice to God did something to make up for one's former disobedience; it was a mark of repentance and an assurance of our good intentions. Sometimes a sacrifice was seen as a gift which might placate God's anger or as a bribe which would persuade him to do what was wanted. But the highest object of sacrifice was to obtain a union with God through sharing a meal with him.

These religious ideas of the meaning of sacrifice are rooted in the nature of man. He exists to love and to be loved. If we are deprived of love our humanity is damaged and diminished. Loving is expressed by giving. The depth of our love is shown by the cost and costliness of our gifts – not their cost in money but their cost for us, as the widow's mite was a giving of all that she had to give. Loving and giving are brought together in the basic Christian text in John 3:16: 'God so loved the world that he gave his only begotten son . . .' Selfishness and sin always hinder the free flow of loving and giving, and the giving which is obstructed becomes sacrificial. When God's act of pure love encountered man's sin, it became the costly sacrifice of the passion and death of Christ on the cross.

We speak of sacrificial giving in a secular sense. In human relationships we give costly gifts which express our love. We may sacrifice time or privacy or prejudice to gain unity with others. Each side gives something. In international relations too each side must give up something if countries are to reach unity; there must be some sacrifice of armaments or of economic gain or territorial claims. Sacrifice is basic to the unity of person with person, and of persons with God. And it is natural to humankind to make costly sacrifices: parents stint themselves to educate their children, or children to provide a home for their aged parents. People sacrifice a kidney or bone-marrow to help others. A man may lose his life in the cause of medical research, or in rescuing someone from a burning building. Such sacrifices can be wasted; the child refuses to work, the old parents refuse to move, the transplant does not take, and money and lives are lost without result. Sacrifices were made in good faith but without the response which would have obtained the end in view. It is true of the sacrifice of Christ on the cross. It was made for all men everywhere but not all men avail themselves of its benefit.

To understand the sacrifice of Christ we must look back to the Old Testament. The Jews used sacrifice to seal and celebrate all sorts of occasions: morning and evening, seedtime and harvest, marriage and birth, and the call to repentance. They believed God required sacrifices, and I believe that he was leading them to an understanding that he expected them to give him of their best. They were to give, for instance, a lamb without blemish of the first year. It was no good trying to foist off God with something inferior.

When God had established this way of sacrifice as right and proper, he revealed more that lay behind the demand for a perfect offering. The prophets came thundering along with their message of the true sacrifice which God required. Note for example Isaiah 1:13:

Bring no more vain oblations; incense is an abomination to me; the new moons and sabbaths, the calling of assemblies, I cannot away with; it is iniquity, even the solemn meetings. Your new moons and your appointed feasts my soul hateth; they are a trouble unto me; I am weary to bear them. And when ye spread forth your hands, I will hide mine eyes from you; yea, when ye make many prayers, I will not hear: your hands are full of blood . . .

– that is, the blood of the sacrifices. And Micah 6:6–8:

Wherewith shall I come before the Lord, and bow myself before the high God? Shall I come before him with burnt offerings, with calves of a year old? Will the Lord be pleased with thousands of rams, or with ten thousand rivers of oil? Shall I give my firstborn for my transgression, the fruit of my body for the sin of my soul? He hath showed thee, O man, what is good; and what doth the Lord require of thee, but to do justly and to love mercy and to walk humbly with thy God.

The prophets are telling us that God does not want the usual sacrificial gifts, however good they may be. He is saying, 'What I want is YOU, yourselves, your souls and bodies. And I require you to be perfect, without spot or blemish of sin.' And that is a sacrifice which man cannot give, 'For all have sinned, and come short of the glory of God' (Rom. 3:23). Even if I were able to determine to live without sin in the future my past sin could not be undone. Only one man, only Jesus Christ, can give God what he requires; He is Son of Man and Son of God, the bridge between God and man. He can bridge the gap of sin between man and God. He comes with the good news that his perfect life may be given for me. In the words of consecration, 'This is my body which is given for you' and 'This is my blood which is shed for you', we have an echo which links the sacrifices of the past with the sacrifice of Christ and with the Mass.

Jesus is man, perfect as man was meant to be. He is also God, the infinite Son of God himself. His sacrifice is of infinite value and available for everyone at all times everywhere. It is available for us and for the whole creation whose priests we are, for 'the whole creation groaneth and travaileth in pain together until now . . . waiting for the adoption, to wit, the redemption . . .' (Rom. 8:22–3). All things wait for us to appropriate the sacrifice to ourselves for our redemption and recreation. As we praise God in the Mass we become the spokesmen of all his inarticulate creation. We speak for all the works of the Lord which the 'Benedicite' charges to bless the Lord, to 'praise him and magnify him for ever'. We should become spokesmen too for those of our human brothers and sisters who have no true idea of God and can only cry out in agony and desolation. As Jesus intercedes for us in heaven we parallel and support his intercession here on earth, offering the Mass on behalf of some person or some cause.

Jesus alone can make atonement because he is the atonement – the at-onement of God and man. We can share in this in the Lord's Supper. I have said that if two parties are to reach unity each will sacrifice something. If God is to meet us he must come down to our level, for we cannot rise to his. We can only 'lift up our eyes to the hills' or, like Isaiah, catch the distant song of angels singing 'Holy, holy, holy'.

But God sacrifices something. That is presumably what is meant by that extraordinary text: 'He emptied himself and took upon him the form of a servant being made in the likeness of man' (Phil. 2:7). Theologians have pondered about its meaning. Clearly Christ did not empty himself of his divine nature, because the whole point of the incarnation is that the total nature of man is united in one person with the total nature of God. But he seems to have divested himself of some aspects and manifestations of divinity. He came without splendour or thundering power.

The incarnation itself is the great act of sacrifice. Death on the cross is the climax and culmination of the sacrifice. His cry, 'It is finished,' at his death, marked the completion of Christ's identification of God and man. But it is the total act of incarnation – his birth and his life, his resurrection and ascension – which is his saving act. It is that which we appropriate to ourselves in and through the Mass.

The Church has never fully explained or understood what the atonement is, or how it attains its end. But all Christians seem agreed that it is wrought in Christ. We reach out into God's glory to try to understand it. 'God was in Christ reconciling the world unto himself.' In the crucifixion God was doing something that only he could do. God does not need to be reconciled to us for he is love, and totally well-disposed towards us. It is we who need to be changed and reconciled, and only Christ, God in man, can do that.

I don't want to discuss the vast doctrine of the atonement but to stress the place which sacrifice plays in the work of atonement and in the way we receive the 'inestimable benefits of his passion' in the Lord's Supper. Scripture shows that, though Christ procured redemption once for all upon the cross, yet something remains to be done for us. 'He ever liveth to make intercession for us' (Heb. 7:25), 'Christ, who is at the right hand of God, intercedes for us' (Rom. 8:34). The picture is of Christ, 'the great high priest of our profession' (Heb. 3:1), entering into the holy place in heaven to plead for us, his once-achieved sacrifice. The sacrifice was completed on the cross but needs, like all sacrifices, to be applied and appropriated. That is what our Lord is doing in heaven. We echo and reflect it when we celebrate the Lord's Supper on earth.

You should read and re-read the Epistle to the Hebrews, and study its relationship with the Old Testament accounts of the Day of Atonement. The Jewish rite foreshadows the great Day of Atonement, Good Friday, when atonement is made for all mankind. The idea is probably best conveyed for most of us in the hymn:

> Once, only once, and once for all,
>   His precious life he gave;
> Before the Cross in faith we fall.
>   And own it strong to save.

> 'One offering, single and complete,'
>   With lips and hearts we say;
> But what he never can repeat
>   He shows forth day by day.

> For as the priest of Aaron's line
>   Within the Holiest stood,
> And sprinkled all the mercy-shrine
>   With sacrificial blood;

> So he who once atonement wrought,
>   Our Priest of endless power,
> Presents himself for those he bought
>   In that dark noontide hour.

His Manhood pleads where now it lives
    On heaven's eternal throne,
And where in mystic rite he gives
    Its Presence to his own.

And so we show thy Death, O Lord,
    Till thou again appear;
And feel, when we approach thy board,
    We have an altar here.

                    (W. Bright)

The Israelites' Day of Atonement helps our understanding of the Lord's Supper, so does their Feast of the Passover. The Jewish religion was the womb from which both our Saviour Christ himself and the Christian faith were born, and the more we learn of the Jewish faith, the more we see how the ancient promises of God are fulfilled in the Church. The celebration of Passover, the central act of Judaism through the ages, commemorates the Exodus from the years of slavery in Egypt. Exodus 12 tells how God sent his angel to bring death to every household in Egypt as a final plague, a final hammer blow, through which Pharoah would be compelled to 'let my people go'. The Israelites were told to take a lamb for every household, to kill it and splash the blood over the lintel of the door. The angel of death would see the blood and pass over that household; its members would be saved from death by the blood of the lamb. This foreshadows John 1:29, where John the Baptist hails Jesus, as the 'Lamb of God', and says to his disciples, 'Behold the Lamb of God which takes away the sin of the world.'

From John's words the anthem is derived which has a place in most liturgies: 'O Lamb of God that takest away the sins of the world, have mercy upon us . . .' (ASB, Rite B). Here we address our Lord in heaven remembering also the picture in Revelation 5:6: 'I beheld, and lo! in the midst of the throne . . . stood a lamb as it had been slain.' We on earth and they in heaven have in common the perfect sacrifice of the Lamb of God who was slain for us upon the cross.

There is a third Old Testament theme which is echoed in the

liturgy. Abraham believed that God wanted him to sacrifice his son Isaac. As they neared the place appointed, Isaac said, 'Father, behold the fire and the wood, but where is the lamb for a burnt offering?' To which Abraham replies, 'My son, God will provide himself a lamb' (Gen. 22:8). These are words of prophecy for they foreshadow the event in which God did, in Jesus, provide the only lamb who could make a 'full, perfect and sufficient sacrifice'.

In looking at the Old Testament stories it is important to remember that the Jews closely identified blood with life. When blood flows away, life flows away. Jesus's words, 'This is my blood which is shed for you,' have exactly the same meaning as, 'This is my life which is given for you.' John's Gospel emphasizes the way in which Jesus chose the 'hour' at which he should 'lay down his life' (John 10:17 ff.). He chose that the crucifixion should be at the time of the Passover and that the Last Supper should be tied together with both. They were tied together in time and tied together by Christ's use of sacrificial language in his institution of the supper which we are commanded to do in remembrance of him. Christ identified himself with the Passover lamb, and the early Church proclaimed this: 'Christ our Passover is sacrificed for us' (1 Cor. 5:7).

God's longing for his people is a strong theme running through the Old Testament. This is paralleled by the strong longing of Jesus when he says that with desire he has desired to eat this Passover with his disciples. It was to be his last Passover meal with them, and immensely more: it was to be the sign of his new covenant with them through the on-going years and the means of his continuing communion and presence with them. The Lord's Supper was to be the means by which 'his one true pure immortal sacrifice' would be available to all men everywhere. His 'desire to eat this Passover with you' was expressed to his disciples and applied especially to the Last Supper itself; but we can legitimately apply his words to every act of Holy Communion. We take communion not just because we wish to receive him, but because he desires to receive us.

We do not know exactly what Christ's words meant when he

said, 'This is my body,' and, 'This is my blood'; but they have a clear meaning for us, even if we cannot totally define it. I hold that Jesus meant what he said: 'This is my body,' means that the bread is his body. Exactly how we are to understand this we simply do not know. It at least means, 'This is the means by which I choose to manifest myself to you.' Or it may mean something even more than that.

I recommend Jesus' teaching about the bread of life in John 6:32–60. You would do well to read it as you prepare for communion. He says there, 'I am the bread of life,' and, 'I am the living bread,' and, 'He that eateth of this bread shall live for ever'. When Jesus taught, 'Except ye eat the flesh of the Son of man and drink his blood ye have no life in you,' then, John reports, 'From that time many of his disciples went back and walked no more with him.' Jesus did not call them back, or say, 'Ah! I only meant it symbolically.' He did not mean it symbolically. He meant it and means it really. And that has been a dividing line in the story of the Church. It has tended to separate most tragically Catholic and Protestant. And it is a dividing line in the personal history of many of us Christians as we come from a consideration of the Holy Communion as simply a means of communing with God to a realization that it is a great deal more than that.

There is a famous verse about this doctrine of the Real Presence which is attributed to Queen Elizabeth I:

> Christ was the Word that spake it;
> He took the bread and break it;
> and what that Word did make it;
> That I believe and take it.

Exactly so!

9

The prayer of intercession

Our prayers are not just a private affair between the individual and God. I believe that they have a deep effect on the world around us. Every day I stand at the altar at St Vedast's and celebrate the Eucharist. As I prepare I form an intention, in other words I say, 'Look God, this is what I want this Mass to be about, this is what I am doing it for.' I bring before God three sets of people. First I bring before him those who attend the church, those who worship here on weekdays and Sundays. I may not remember all their names, but I don't think God needs to have them all ticked off in his diary – he knows who they are. I do mention some that I know have particular troubles. Secondly I remember the few, mostly caretakers and pub-keepers, who live in my particular city parish. Then I bring before God the great number of people who work within the parish; I pray for all, whether they are Christians, Jews, Muslims, Buddhists, or atheists, or nothing; all who work within the area that is allotted to me. I also say to God, 'Look, I want not only these people to benefit at Mass but all those whom they are concerned with, their sick and troubled and anxious ones.' I don't know who they are, but I specifically offer the Holy Sacrament for all these people in the belief that they are, as it were, lifted up one-thousandth of an inch from being bogged down in the earthiness of things. I believe that we all in our prayers and adoration can lift the world and all its people up towards God so that his power can heal and love them all.

God loves us and is aware of our every need. Why then should we have to ask for anything? First, because this is what our deepest instincts tell us to do. If you find yourself in desperate danger, or if someone whom you love is facing a serious operation, you will not sit passively rapt in silent meditation; you are driven to express your need. And it is impossible to think of God as a loving Father without asking him for the things we need. Also, Jesus laid constant emphasis on the need to ask. 'Ask and ye shall receive. Seek and ye shall find. Knock and it shall be opened unto you.' He offered his own petitions to God. Remember that in the Garden of Gethsemane he prayed 'Father, let this cup pass from me.' And he interceded for Simon – 'I have prayed that thy faith fail not.' (It is worth noting, and relevant to our own experience, that neither of these prayers was granted – at least not in the short run.)

Our Lord habitually required people to express their needs to him. Day by day, Jesus walked through the cities of Galilee, through the streets of Jerusalem, past the gates of the Temple where the blind and the crippled and the maimed thronged in expectation of help from passers-by. But he carried on walking and took no notice until someone called out and asked for help. Blind Bartimeus is a case in point. 'What do you want me to do for you?' says Jesus, although one would have thought that the need was obvious. 'Lord, let me receive my sight.' Then, after the petition has been formulated, the healing power of Jesus springs into action. On only one occasion did Jesus seek out a sick person and heal him, and that was the rather discouraged individual by the pool of Bethesda who did not have any friends or any faith.

Some kinds of prayer seem to link us with the faith of other religions, but our intercession is essentially Christian. Only the Christian understands the need for intercession and the power of it. There are other great religions with great qualities – Buddhism, for example, looks on evil with great compassion, but it does not look beyond the evil with the kind of hope with which the Christian looks beyond evil; for the Christian looks towards its ultimate conquest through the will of God and the power of Christ, and by the help of our prayers.

We believe that God uses our petition and intercession; through it we release his power to change people and to change situations. We ally ourselves with him that good may flow. It is obvious enough that God uses the minds of scientists, philosophers, poets, and saints to change lives and situations and concepts about the world. He uses the hands of artists, musicians and doctors to create and heal and renew. If God uses human minds and hands, then surely he will also use the spiritual power of human prayers to change and heal.

How does one pray for others? We do not need to use many words or to explain things in detail. We are not giving God news about the unfortunate man in hospital; God is aware of his plight. We are not trying to inform God, nor to get him on our side; we are trying to get on his side, to align ourselves with him so that his healing love can flow through us. When a sick man's friends tore up the roof and let their friend down through it, they were not just trying to inform Jesus about him but were putting him in contact with the power of God. So when we pray for others we try to bring them in line with God and to remove the blockages which prevent the influx of his loving will. When you know of a situation of need or pain or hunger, or you just want to pray for someone you love, try to put yourself in his situation, stand beside him, hold him to you and cry out with him, on his behalf. Cry, 'Lord, have mercy,' and try to share his suffering or need and to lift him up to the power of love. 'Father, help.'

I find it useful to keep a list of people for whom I need and want to pray, so that I do not waste time trying to remember them, and do not forget to pray for someone for whom it may be vital. Do remember that almost everyone knows someone who has no one else to pray for them. Your prayer may be essential in such a case, and God may be longing for someone to open a channel for his love so that he can heal that person. Your prayers are necessary and if you will not bother to intercede you are refusing someone a source of strength and help. Consider this world in the present day – the fear, the starvation, the many kinds of distress, and our terrifying weakness. Some of the trouble exists because Christians are too damned lazy to pray – and I mean that literally.

Jesus loves the whole world and our concern should reach

out towards the evil and horror of the whole world. Whatever our own state and the darkness of our time, God is there and able to reveal himself. If we stay looking and leaning towards him and trying to join the cry of adoration which goes up from the whole company of heaven, our adoration becomes shot with intercession. Christ is the King of Glory of the Psalms and the glorious rider on the white horse in Revelation; but between those he is the King on the cross, the King of the outcast, the dispossessed, the failures, the despised. He is the King who weeps and agonizes over the pain of the world. If we are to serve him as King it is our job to share his intercession, forcing ourselves to look at suffering and standing with Christ in his pain and his longing. It means hearing the cries of the helpless and hopeless, joining them with Christ's cry of dereliction on the cross.

Remember the atom bomb that dropped on Hiroshima – on August 6th, the Feast of the Transfiguration. Remember how on the mountain of the transfiguration there was a cloud and within it the light burst and blazed forth from Jesus. It wasn't that he was under some kind of light coming down from heaven upon him; the light shone forth from him; he was the centre. I don't believe that God willed that that bomb should be dropped, but that, in his providence, he said, 'If you are going to drop that damn thing, do it on the Feast of the Transfiguration – and I'll have something to say about it.' So it dropped. There was the great mushroom cloud, the cloud of death and devastation. Everyone within reach of it died or was deformed and twisted. Every thing within reach was twisted and turned and moved out of shape. Not only at that time but for a generation, and for generations after, twisted beings suffered and will suffer from the awful thing. And remember that that atom bomb was a tiny bomb compared with the hellish horrors which now stand waiting in the wings. It seems to me that what our Lord, what God, is saying is, 'Look, now hold together these two clouds, the cloud of the transfiguration and the cloud of the horror of death, the black cloud of death and the bright cloud of glory.' The transfiguration shows that behind the dark cloud there shines the bright one. And the crucifixion makes an even deeper statement: within the destruction and devastation, within the agony, there is Christ. The acts of God through history, back to the Exodus, proclaim that only the acts of God can deliver. Our most treasured possessions are facts of history – the incarnation, the transfiguration, the crucifixion, the resurrection; only as we hold to these can we face the world's insanity.

When we think of the insanity, sin, and horrors of life today, we realize how little the Church is when it is set against them. It is a little like salt in the stew or like the leaven in the loaf. It is the work of leaven to lift up, and one work of salt is to prevent things from going bad. This is the work of intercession – to lift things up and to prevent them from going bad. The salt of prayer does something to disinfect the world's infectious insanity. The intercessor helps to bring the will of God to bear on the forces of evil. He mediates, he comes between. He interferes in the name of God to free and enable the will of God by standing with it. Only the sanity and love of our prayers will enable the course of history to be changed from the horror which waits in the wings to a state which sanity and love can permeate.

The Church is small but ought all the same to exercise power, God's power, through its prayers. There are places where monks and nuns exercise this power through prayer and reparation; but this ought not to be left to convents and so on; it is a work which ought to be practised much more widely by ordinary members of the Church. Sometimes this work is done by older people. When they are no longer working actively in their professions they may discover that they need God and have time to give to him. They may be late in answering God's call to work in his vineyard, but, through their intercession, they may do their most valuable work for him at this late hour. Some are able to use in prayer the insights which their life work has given to them; perhaps experience has helped them to understand the tensions of the Third World or the diabolical dimensions of our own society. They can hear the cries of despair from the helpless, the hopeless, and the inarticulate, and lift them to the heart of God. Sometimes those facing sickness and pain and the limitations of old age are able to offer these to our Lord in association with his own suffering on man's behalf, and in this they learn a deeper understanding of his work.

Intercession of any kind is setting ourselves alongside God against the powers of evil – against the deadness and disintegration and despair. Like all coming to grips with evil it is bound to be costly if it is to be effective. The cross shows us that the cutting edge of prayer lies in sacrifice. If I really mean that I offer my prayer 'through Jesus Christ our Lord', I am talking about the cross, and it isn't much good talking about the cross unless I am doing something about the cross. I believe that if I am really praying for someone I must accompany that prayer by some personal sacrifice of fasting or discipline. Where possible I must make the effort to do something practical about those for whom I pray. People sometimes think of prayer as a turning away from the real world of action, but true intercession may clear our vision and sensitize our consciences and send us out in love and obedience to stand up against some wrong, or to get to know some unpopular person, or to give time to some difficult demanding cause. We must be ready to speak and act for others if we offer ourselves as channels through which the love and power of God may flow towards them.

There are times when we are able to sense clearly that we ourselves are receiving the support of other people's prayers. When I found myself cut off from all natural human contact in the prison cells of the South African Security Police I did not know how far the news of my arrest had spread. Yet, when I went through the words of the Mass – without bread and without wine – I was vividly aware of the whole company of heaven and of those whom Jesus loves on earth. Although I was in solitary confinement, I have never had such a sense of belonging in all my life. That sense of being with the company of Christ's beloved cannot, it seems to me, have been due to anything other than the prayers of thousands of people, prayers which were being said for me in churches all over the world. Their prayers were seeping through the concrete walls of my cell and filling the place with love. I wrote in my prison diary:

'I had the feeling this morning that there were thousands of Christians throughout the world with me – a most extraordinary, glorious, truly comforting and strengthening feeling.'

Sometimes people suggest that intercession is just something which people can do if they are too infirm or too busy to do anything else. But intercession is a high and demanding calling. Christ himself 'ever liveth to make intercession'. What vocation could be higher than that of sharing in the work of the risen Christ?

10

The prayer of adoration

Broadly speaking 'adoration' covers all kinds of praise or worship in which we laud God for what he is. Here I want to use the word more precisely for a particular kind of prayer, and I must make clear what I mean. I must distinguish 'adoration' from 'meditation' and 'contemplation'. These are good, valid words which have been used by some of the greatest spiritual writers and given clear meanings. Unfortunately they have been used, lately especially, by people who are not great masters of prayer and who have given them wider or rather different meanings. That is why I prefer the word 'adoration' for the kind of prayer which I try to practise and will try to describe. Father Arthur Stanton wrote: 'Meditation is a detachment from the things of the world in order to attend to the things of God. Contemplation is a detachment from the things of God in order to attend to God himself.' That definition of contemplation describes what I mean by adoration, but the words have been used differently as I shall show.

Strictly speaking, meditation – in the traditional Christian sense – is not prayer but one of the gateways to prayer. For the Christian the most common form of meditation is to take a verse or incident from the Bible, generally a passage about Jesus, and to 'read, mark, learn and inwardly digest it'. One is taught to 'read, picture, ponder and pray'. The traditional (Ignatian) method of meditation can be quite difficult for people with little imagination. The Bible is a series of books which the Holy Spirit has breathed into, and we ask the Spirit to breathe some of the inspiration he put there out of its pages and into us. There is something hidden there for you and me.

We take the word of Scripture, turn it over, consider it, hold
it in mind as long as we like. That, hopefully, will lead us to
prayer, to the I-and-Thou encounter with God, and we can put
the Bible down gently when it has done its job. Meditation on
the life and teaching of Jesus is practised by most Christians in
some form or other.

But today we often hear of non-Christian forms of meditation, like 'transcendental meditation'. This expression covers
a multitude of techniques of spiritual experience or psychological growth. When they are taught by a disciplined,
devotional person, who is well-versed in these methods, they
can do a great deal of good. But I have been warned by a
Buddhist monk of some standing that many teachers of TM in
the Western world are not so qualified.

I do believe that the best Eastern mystics do have something
valuable to teach us about techniques in prayer. In particular
they can tell us a good deal about the relationship between the
body and the soul, or spirit, in prayer. It is we who pray, not
just our souls. The body is important too. It helps if we use a
posture which helps us to relax yet keep attentive. The rhythm
of breathing can be particularly important to Christians to
whom the Spirit is the Breath of God. Christian writers,
especially some who have lived in India, have written usefully
about these things. One is Father Slade ssje of Anchorhold.

The followers of TM like to bandy round words like 'mantra'
and 'mandala'. It is worth noticing that the ideas which they
represent are not peculiar to the Eastern religions. Christians
also have their mantras, the potent words which we repeat over
and over. We have the different names of God, like El Shaddai,
Adonai, Immanuel. We have the Jesus Prayer which consists
in repeating the words 'Lord Jesus Christ, Son of the living
God, have mercy upon me, a sinner' – or some variation of
this. We have our mandalas, that is the objects which may help
us in prayer, our crosses and crucifixes, our icons and rosaries.
We do not use the Eastern words but some of our practices
are not unlike.

Though the religions of East and West have plenty of
common ground, they do not use the word 'meditation' in the

same way. Not only is their meditation not based on the Bible but it is less active, more passive than ours. Nor do they use the word 'contemplation' in our way, so there is a danger nowadays of confusing Christian contemplation with non-Christian ways of prayer. The non-Christian forms were not so familiar in the days when the great teachers of prayer, like St John of the Cross and St Teresa, wrote their great books in which contemplation means the highest and greatest kind of prayer. For them it is a quiet relationship with God in which there may be an element of 'given' experience in which it is not we but the Spirit who take the initiative. I do not want to detract from or to discard anything the great mystics have said, but I want to use 'adoration' in place of 'contemplation' to distinguish our practice from that of others who use the word contemplation in their own senses.

Let me illustate its non-Christian use. It is a practice for some Eastern mystics to contemplate their navels. Presumably 'contemplate' here means to gaze at and consider deeply that which is contemplated. The navel is for these mystics a very real matter for contemplation and can lead them to great heights and depths. My navel is that which once connected me to my mother and so through her to all living things and to life itself. The umbilical cord is cut and so the navel is that also which separates me from all creation, and marks the beginning of me, myself. All this can lead to contemplation of true reality, of the meaning and wonder of life and being; but it has not necessarily anything to do with God. Many of these mystics do not believe in God and almost certainly not in a personal God. Then ordinary men and women may contemplate beautiful things and find something there which speaks to them of reality and truth; but not necessarily of God. Christian prayer implies a relationship, and relationships can only exist between persons. In prayer there is a relationship between me and the Persons of the Trinity. We can contemplate persons but we can also contemplate things, with which we cannot make relationships. It may be profitable to contemplate one's navel, but it is hardly possible to enter into a relationship with it! So the word 'contemplation' can be confusing and I prefer to use 'adoration'.

I also like the word 'adoration' because it suggests movement. I have already mentioned Augustine's famous saying: 'Thou hast made our hearts for thee and they are restless until they rest in thee.' The Latin is important: our hearts are made *ad te*, towards thee, and they are restless until they rest *in te*. Adoration implies a movement towards God in whom alone we can find our rest and our fulfilment. Contemplation, it seems to me, can be a static thing while adoration cannot be. It reaches out, or it reaches in, towards God. It is ever seeking and ever searching for him for whom 'my soul has a desire and a longing'.

In reaching towards God we seek a sense of his presence. God can and does vouchsafe to make his presence known at any place at any time, but some places have a specially holy or numinous feeling which we may sense. Churches where the sacraments have been celebrated over the centuries have this sense of God's presence, and at every communion God is particularly present. The Bible constantly depicts God's presence as being, as it were, hidden by a gentle cloud, lest we are blinded by his glory. We experience God through some kind of cloud, yet there are thin places in it and, with one sense or another, we may discern God's presence and feel that he beckons us.

The life of prayer can be conceived in two ways: both as God's search and longing for us, and as our search and longing for him. I believe that the first aspect of the spiritual life is very much disregarded. We are seeking and searching for God; but he beckons us and invites us, and longs for us to come into his presence to share his love. It is he who draws us. His love for us comes first, not our desire and longing for him, though that will come. He does not need us, but he does desire us.

How then can we progress towards the prayer of adoration? We need to heighten our awareness of God in everything. We need to notice the glimpses we have of his nature in beautiful things. We need to see not only 'tongues in trees, books in the running brooks, sermons in stones,' but 'God in everything'.

We need also to notice his word to us in things which are ugly or inconvenient. It is easy to see a passing ambulance, or a police car with its siren blaring, as a prompter to intercession. It is not so easy to be aware of God in telephone calls, or door bells, or the noises of city life, or in those people whom we find a nuisance. Awareness of God is the background to adoration.

This awareness should change our whole attitude to people, not least to ourselves. If we try to see the hand of God in everything that happens, and in everyone whom we know and meet, we shall become more loving, more understanding and more compassionate. I hesitate to say 'more tolerant'; we may become less impatient with things – a typewriter that sticks or a car that will not start – but a Christian must not be tolerant of cruelty or injustice. Adoration should throw us back into the world in such a state of flaming love that we will not tolerate these things.

Our growing awareness of God and our increasing consistency in our attitude towards him is, as it were, the stage on which our periods of formal adoration can be set. However much we become aware of God and learn to love him in and through everything and everyone, we do still need to put aside periods of time in which we attempt simply to adore God and to do nothing else. These times will vary enormously according to our vocation and circumstances, but they must happen.

I have mentioned the Little Brothers of Jesus and the Little Sisters, who have what they call 'the hour'. Although they go out to work in the world, they are bound to set aside an hour every day for adoration, even though it may well have to be in the middle of the night. They are taught in their novitiate that this hour is not a time for 'saying their prayers'. If they have to pray for others, or confess their sins, or ask that they grow in grace, they must find another time for doing that. 'The hour' is for giving their full attention to God. And that is very, very difficult. I attempt to practise the hour myself each day and, since I almost never succeed in keeping it 'for God, for him alone', I know just how difficult it is; yet I am certain that the attempt is very worthwhile.

I do believe that an hour is the right amount of time to try

to give to adoration. Many people obviously, especially those
with family commitments, will not be able to do this; but one
cannot get into adoration deeply in less time than that. Of
course, because God is love, moments of adoration do come,
they are given to us from time to time as it were instan-
taneously. They still need time for savouring, for absorbing,
and for maturing. I think that, if one can find one solid hour
in the week, that is better than scattering short periods through
the week.

So one finds a time and puts it aside for God. One becomes
relaxed and attentive, for this is the natural combination of
attitudes in which to listen to one whom one loves. Then one
finds some place from which to begin the movement of adoration. Some people use objects: a lighted candle, a bowl of
water, a crucifix or picture of the crucifixion. Some like something to touch which helps their awareness of God: beads, a
pebble from the beach, something with a special feel like silk
or old porcelain. Your starting place may be personal, but of
course the greatest treasure house of starting places is the Bible.

What kind of passage from the Bible can help us towards
adoration? I find it best not to use a passage with which I am
too familiar or about which I have already formed ideas. We
may have heard the miracles and parables of Jesus expounded
so often that they have lost their impact. Also, they tend,
rightly, to lead to meditation rather than to adoration. Some
of the great proclamations of our Lord, such as 'I am the Light
of the world' (John 8:12), are obvious starting places. One
needs something with a devotional rather than an intellectual
content, that is something which clearly reaches out beyond
the grasp of the intellect, like 'I am Alpha and Omega' (Rev.
1:8). Many parts of Revelation are useful, but on the whole I
find verses from the Psalms more valuable than any other
biblical material. One wants something which is emotive in the
sense that it moves our hearts and minds towards God. Adoration is not finally a matter of the emotions; but the emotions
do move the will and it is right that they should be used in that
way. Besides the Bible we may turn to Christian writers and

poets for help in building up a personal treasure house of phrases which can help us.

Here are some samples from the words which have helped me:
'Behold, he has made all things new.'
'Christ is our corner-stone.'
'My God and my all.'
'Who is the King of Glory? The Lord of Hosts, he is the King of Glory.'
'My beloved is mine and I am his.'
'He is the light of the world.'
'My rock and my fortress.'
'Underneath are the everlasting arms.'
'O praise God in his holiness.'
We may prefer to use single words: 'Jesus', 'Father', 'Master'.

As adoration is simply love it is very hard to describe. What I try to do is to follow the practice of the Little Brothers and Sisters of Jesus who try to look and listen and long for God, leaning towards him in love. One may begin by looking or listening to something, trying to look through this something to God who created it and holds it in being, trying to hear God himself through words which echo his voice. So one leans out towards him or seeks him within one's own heart. We reach out towards that central point of love where 'our lives are hid with Christ in God'.

Our leaning is accompanied by longing. We long for God himself – not for what he can give, not even for his peace, but simply for him. This is almost impossible to describe, because inevitably we do long for what he has to give, but one has to press gently through that longing for his gifts, towards God himself. One longs for love, but love is not just a gift from God: because God is love, to long for his love is to long for God himself. And we must go on longing long. God cannot be hurried. We may have to spend all our adoration-time just in this longing. We may have to spend many such times. It may be a long time before anything seems to happen. But the time is not wasted; something is happening. If we are longing for him we are maturing and being made ready for love. We are increasing our capacity for love, our *capax dei*. God is preparing us to bear the revelation of love.

Love is the point, the object of prayer. 'The hour'– or whatever time we have put aside for this – is, as I have said, 'for him' and not for ourselves. But because he is love he desires to share his life and love with us. When we are ready he will give us that love. I want to stress that love is given, not gained or gotten. It is not a question of being worthy; no one is ever worthy. Our growth in love is a process with seed-time, growth, and harvest; spring, summer, autumn and winter. Our capacity for the love and knowledge of God grows under his hands. These given moments of love come when we are ready. He gives his love, himself, in as far as we are able to receive at that time. When he gives he floods us with a love that is wholly undeserved and indeed inexplicable and inexpressible. It is always true that 'We are his and he is ours for ever', but the realization that this is so is what is given in adoration. The revelation of God's love may be only a momentary realization but it is real and unmistakeable. We can savour it and take the joy and the memory of it with us into our lives and into the world.

I must be careful to complement what I have said by adding that the revelation of love is not by any means all sweetness and light. The nature of God's love lies in the cross, and in our adoration the cross and the passion of our Lord will often be our focus. I cannot speak of this with great reality because I am still at the edge of love; but I strongly commend to you that you should read the *Revelations of Divine Love* by Julian of Norwich; she writes from the centre of it all and will show you what I mean.

The saints have spoken of a time when the journey of adoration, the journey towards God, comes to its fulfilment, the rest in God. In one sense, since God is infinite and I am finite, I think that the journey will never end; I imagine that the never-ending journey into love is one of the joys of heaven. But I think it is also clear that the journey into love can find its fulfilment, at least temporarily, here on earth. I know this, not from my own experience, but from that of the great mystical writers. I have not found their fulfilment, though I would like to find it: and perhaps this is where I go wrong, because it is not a matter of finding it but of finding him. Jesus himself said, 'Abide in me and I in you.' That is the ultimate, the only thing that matters. Since he said it to his disciples while he and they were on the earth it must be possible for us to have that abiding, and to rest in God here and now.

11

The way of loneliness

Some years ago, in what was then Salisbury in Rhodesia, I used to help in training the suicide service, the Samaritans. An authoritative textbook which we read said this about suicides: 'A major factor is the lack of supportive acceptance of an individual by his social group' – that is to say, the person who commits suicide is generally lonely. It is true in my experience that really devastating loneliness can lead to suicide, because, in general, men and women are not meant to live alone.

Yet I am sure that some people are meant to live alone. There are a growing number of vocations to the eremitical life (that is, the life of a hermit). Probably many more people are called to this life than those who recognize the call. Those who do realize that this is their vocation, instead of going off to live in caves as they did in the old days, now often go off to live in caravans. There are a number of them over the world and quite a number here in England. And there are others who are learning to live in solitude, not in a physical desert, but in cities. People like de Foucauld and the Little Brothers of Jesus (such as Jean Voilleaume and Carlo Caretto) have said that today the basic desert is the city. It is in the city that nothing grows; that there is just emptiness, where nothing really lives; that there is a waste land without love. There is the loneliness of being among crowds of people with whom we have no deep relationships. Yet some can use their own silence and solitude as a means of encounter with reality, with God, for the sake of the surrounding world. There is much pressure nowadays to go out and do something, to use one's time, talent and education to try to patch up the ills of the world. I am thankful that there is also a contrasting movement steering others to hold the world up to God rather than involving themselves over much in its activity. The Little Brothers and Sisters of Jesus, for example, live among the poorest and most deprived people, sharing their life and work but refusing to get caught up in church activity. Their job, they say, is simply to be there, 'to be standing delegates of prayer'. I think that some lay people are called to solitude in the city, to a life of dedicated loneliness.

Amongst the modern people who are learning to live alone there is a group called '*poustiniki*'. These follow an old Russian tradition. Outside any Russian village you may still find a *poustinia*, a bare wooden hut where a hermit, man or woman, may live. The *poustinik* may spend years there or may stay for a short time only. In the hut is a mattress, a table and chair, a cup, a jug, a pallet, a Bible, an icon, and a bare cross without a figure. The *poustinik* tries to think of himself as being on the cross in the place of Christ; in silence and simplicity he tries to empty himself of himself so that Christ can take over. He spends time in adoration, and because he is available to God he is available to others also. He is available for those who come to talk about their troubles or about the things of God; they can bring something to eat or share food from his little vegetable plot. One of his rules is that the door may never be locked; he is available to any villager who comes for help of any kind at any hour of day or night. He is called away from his prayer or his reading if the farmer needs help with the harvest, if the postman can't deliver the letters, or if a woman needs some repairs done or some help in sickness. He goes to help, generally with manual work, and then gets back to his private place and the work of offering himself for the world in prayer. This Russian concept was brought to the West by Catherine de Hueck Docherty who came from Russia in 1920, a penniless refugee with a sick husband and a small child. Over the years she has helped to develop a new concept of the lay apostolate in Canada and the USA, and also here in the UK. I think we should watch what is happening and see if it has something to say to us.

Someone who has written about the *poustiniki* says this: 'Many people do not realize that their loneliness is an invitation to share in the loneliness of God.' Our loneliness may hold that invitation to share with Christ in his rejection by the world at large, to share something of the experiences of Gethsemane and Golgotha. We may also share joyous nights of prayer like those Jesus spent with his Father. We may have to face the loneliness of standing for a principle and being sent to Coventry for it. Some stand which we take may lead to confinement in a police cell. There are many kinds of loneliness which reflect something in the suffering of Christ.

If we can relate our experience to that of Christ it will become more fruitful. Loneliness need not be a devastating, devouring dragon; that depends on the way one faces it. There is an ancient archetypal myth, a theme which is found in many fairy tales. A very ugly being, like a frog or a dragon, is kissed by a princess and then turns into something beautiful. I believe that the dragon of loneliness can turn into a darling thing if you choose it and embrace it. As in jujitsu you yield to your attacker in such a way that his impetus is added to your strength, enabling you to throw him over your shoulder, so you can use your threatening loneliness in some positive way. You will mature in solitude if you accept it and learn how to use it.

John Donne said: 'No man is an island entire of itself.' In many towns there are thousands of human islands, and many of them are psychologically separated from each other. There are schizoid characters who cannot make relationships, who – perhaps through no fault of their own – are curled up in themselves, trying to protect themselves like psychological embryos. There are hysterics of the kind who are so hungry for love that they become clinging and devouring and cause others to reject them. There are homosexuals, and others, whose desire for love may run them into destroying jealousies. There are those who dig trenches of selfishness or arrogance round themselves. There are masochists who hold tight to their loneliness and resist every friendly advance that is made towards them; they dig defensive trenches and fill them with tears of self-pity.

Our problems may lie in the fact that we have not chosen to

be alone and so we find it difficult to embrace our loneliness. What of the afflicted, the blind and the deaf? And of course there are the kinds of loneliness that may come upon us all. There is bereavement, where the greater our love for the dead one, the greater the hurt in our loss. There is the loneliness which old age brings as our friends die off and we are left.

I am not sure that all these dragons can be slain. Remember Revelation 12:7–12:

> There was war in heaven: Michael and his angels fought against the dragon; and the dragon fought and his angels . . . And the great dragon . . . was cast out into the earth, and his angels were cast out with him . . . Woe! woe to the inhabiters of the earth and of the sea! for the devil is come down unto you, having great wrath because he knoweth he hath but a short time.

But the time of our distress never seems short; the years of our loneliness seem very long. Some of our dragons have got to be lived with. They must be tamed and domesticated, and that can only be done one day at a time, one night at a time, one weekend at a time.

When I was a very young priest I knew an old priest who had never married. Someone asked him if he had taken a vow of celibacy when he was young. 'Well, no,' he replied, 'I just get up each morning and kneel down and say, "Please God, don't let me get married today!" ' I have found that very helpful! If you look forward to years and years of loneliness, of course you get frightened and depressed; you should just think out how you are going to enjoy your solitude today. We should not think so much of filling our time as of fulfilling it. Ask yourself what you can do this weekend to use it in a productive way.

Another worthwhile saying which I have treasured is, 'To do nothing is very good, but to have nothing to do is very bad.' There is a time for resting completely and doing absolutely nothing. But to have nothing to do is a devastating, destroying thing; I learnt that through being unemployed in the slump in the 1930s when I wasn't wanted by anybody. I learnt it too in solitary confinement. On one day I crawled round the floor of my cell and found some bristles from a broom. I spent a longish time weaving them into a tiny cross, and that was good because I had found something to do.

Another period when I felt lonely was when I was working as organizing secretary of a three-year mission to my diocese. I had no church of my own and preached nearly every Sunday in a different church. There was no one with whom I could talk about my work. I kept sane because I was attached to a covent where there was a daily Mass; and because I belonged to the Society of the Holy Ghost, a small company of unmarried priests who keep a common rule. There are various societies in the Church which can help isolated lay people also to feel that they are praying and working with an invisible company of friends who share their particular aims.

If you cannot embrace solitude, or tame it, or grow through using it, then the first thing to do is to admit that you cannot. Don't pretend that you are not lonely, either to yourself or to other people. Recognize that among Christians there is a spirit called *koinonia*, often translated 'fellowship'. This means that we need and belong to one another. Once one admits one's loneliness within the Christian fellowship then the belonging, the brotherhood, comes into being. It is something given by God when we recognize our needs, a gift which we cannot earn or contrive for ourselves.

Remember St Paul's words: 'Bear ye one another's burdens and so fulfil the law of Christ.' If you see someone who is being destroyed by loneliness – even if they are too proud to admit it – try to go in and share that loneliness. Even lonely people can sometimes find other lonely people and take some of their burden. Look out for some lonely person to cherish, and persist even if, in their pride, they try at first to resist you. 'By this shall all men know that ye are my disciples, that ye love one another.'

12

The way of a depressive

There are periods of darkness and dryness in prayer for nearly everyone. The inability to pray as we used to pray is often a signal to us that God is calling us on to a closer and deeper relation with him. We must press forward through those times when prayer seems meaningless and we begin to wonder whether the whole enterprise has not been a mistake. At such times I find a special value in books of prayers. I can use them, although I do not feel that I really mean them at the time, because I want to mean them and am determined to go on seeking God. I know that he loves me and that if I persevere I shall know his closeness once again.

Though there are likely to be periods of darkness in the experience of any serious Christian, yet there are some for whom darkness is a frequent, persistent torment. I have made it a habit to ask those who come to see me about difficulties with prayer a few questions about their feelings, their sleep pattern and so on, and in many cases it becomes obvious that the real problem is depression. Often such people feel ashamed that they cannot pull themselves out of their depression by prayer and will power. It can be a relief to them to have their feelings recognized and to discuss positive ways of coping with them.

I write from first-hand experience. I get impatient with doctors who ask me what I am depressed about. The person in depression is not necessarily depressed about anything. Everything may seem black, gloomy and hopeless. There is a temptation to contract out, to withdraw from jobs which do not seem worth doing, to want to be alone. There may be the thought of contracting out completely through suicide. One feels physically and mentally weary. One slouches about, feeling lonely and desolate and irrationally angry and touchy with one's closest friends.

In depression we may find out horrible things about ourselves. It rubs one's nose in actual and real guilt, forcing one to look at one's failures and consistent sins, at subtle selfishness, at grossly physical sins, or terrifying hardness of heart.

Because depression raises the question of suicide, it is good to be prepared for this and to have worked out some solid reasons against it which will give you something to hold onto in times of dejection. Suicide is often thought of as 'taking my own life', but my life is not my own: it was given me by God through my parents, and someone took quite a lot of trouble to make sure that I survived and grew up. I am a unique part of the human race and no one else can stand in for me. To kill myself is to say, 'Look, God, you made a mistake and there is nothing you can do about it. My life is a mess beyond all hope. I cannot bear it and you cannot help me.' That is blasphemy. That is turning one's back on the possibility of accepting God's forgiveness and love. It is a rejection too of all those who need me, who love me, or have tried to help me.

It is no good trying to struggle against depression, or getting depressed about being depressed, or angry with one's anger! Easier said than done, I know. But it is better to accept the fact of our depression and seek medical help, if possible from a psychiatrist. You ought not to take risks with depression, as it may be a really serious illness with side-effects on your physical health. It may damage your work and your relationships with those who are close to you. Little as we know about depression, it is known that some types have a physical cause, or can at least be physically alleviated, while others may have a psychological cause which can be got at and dealt with by trained people. While there is no point in living on pills, it is stupid not to use them when they are needed. Some people think it is wrong to take medicine, especially for states which do not appear to have an obvious physical cause; they feel that the grace of God should be sufficient. But it may well be that medicine or skilled treatment will provide the channels for God's grace.

It is not helpful to say that Christians ought not to be depressed. Perhaps it is true, but it's no good telling us not to be what we are! And it's no good trying to cheer up through the jolly books and light-hearted parties which well-meaning friends sometimes provide. It is more helpful to turn to music, or poetry, or books, which echo our mood. It makes us less lonely to know that others have shared our pain – as I have felt the agony of David when he cried out at the death of his son:

> And the king was much moved, and went up to the chamber over the gate, and wept; and as he went, thus he said, O my son Absalom, my son, my son Absalom! would God I had died for thee, O Absalom, my son, my son! (2 Sam. 18:33)

Depression may give Christians an opportunity to discover God in the depths. Both Old and New Testaments have plenty to say about basic emotions which are below conscious control. They use words like 'bowels' and 'reins' (kidneys). 'My heart was grieved,' says the Psalmist, 'It went even through my reins, so foolish was I and ignorant, even as a beast before thee.' The Epistles, in the Authorized Version, several times use the word 'bowels' for feelings too deep for words. The Authorized Version often uses 'the heart' to represent the more conscious, more articulate part of feelings, the ego rather than the id, perhaps. We are told to lift up our hearts, whereas it is inconceivable that we should lift up our guts. But when we are down there in the depths, unable to lift ourselves or to be lifted, God stays with us down there in the depression. He abides in us and we in him, even down there. Indeed in some ways it is easier to find God in the depths than in the heights. 'If I climb up into heaven, thou art there,' is all very well but it does mean climbing, it means discipline and hard work and sacrifice. But 'if I go down into hell, thou art there also'. It does not need any effort to go down. In the sort of hell which depression is, he is certainly there. He may not seem to give any comfort and strength that one can feel consciously, but there is somehow a closeness to reality, to the basic fact of things, which brings one closer to God who is the basic fact of all being.

An analogy which helps me in thinking about this is the neutron star. It burns itself out by throwing off its protons and everything else and thus becomes total emptiness, what is called 'infinite gravity', the dead centre, the total stillness at the heart of the whirlpool which yet sucks in everything around it. This, it seems to me, is the epitome of depression, and in some ways also a picture of the meaning of the cross. It is to that still centre that depression can bring us. Or, to take another analogy, it feels like being buried deep in the soil, where there is no sunlight, or smothered in heavy, wet jungle. These are places where, however dark or dangerous they may be, things do grow. So, although I can hardly welcome being depressed, I keep on hoping that next time it happens, I shall be able to deal with it more positively and that I shall be able to gain something from it and grow in it.

I believe it is essential to keep praying in depression. It is vital to hang on to the lifeline of my normal rule of prayer. Also, as and how I can, I should use my anger and tiredness and despair to realize my total dependence on God. When I feel utterly useless and unable of my own will to do anything at all, I really know from experience, and not just with my intellect, that I do not have any existence except through the continual maintaining and sustaining power of God's love. I am held and cradled in his love – that is what the great poem 'St Patrick's Breastplate' is about:

> Christ be with me, Christ within me,
> Christ behind me, Christ before me . . .

His love penetrates through every fibre of every being – spirit, soul and body – and so all created things, including my empty self, reflect the glory of that love. It may be a dark glory, not glamorous or gorgeous, but it is there within me. I am held in being, sustained and covered by him. So in the hopelessness and meaninglessness and depression, when the guiding beacon of God's glorious transcendence vanishes, it is possible to glimpse the immanence of God within us. It is in the depths that 'our lives are hid with Christ in God'.

The book of Job gives us a magnificent picture of the man who goes through darkness to a sight of God. Job is torn between his faith in God and his own agony of body and soul. In deep despair he calls out against the injustices of God. There come to him four men who have come to be known as 'Job's comforters'. These are like the specialists, the social scientists, the analysts of all sorts, and it is their business to know all the answers. They are obsessed with the necessity of finding the answers; but there aren't any answers, either to the private pain or to the world's massive agonies. Job turns from these spurious specialists to God himself, and screams at him. And God is not there; or so it appears. But when Job has exhausted all his rage, his resentment, and his bitterness on God, then God thunders out, not so much his answer as his defence. He reveals himself by unfolding the immense and blinding splendour of his whole creation. Job begins to see. Not to see the answers – there still aren't any answers – but 'mine eye seeth thee'. And that is all that matters. God doesn't explain suffering. He comes, finally, to share it, as we Christians well know. Read Job. You may find the comforters turgid at times and want to skip them, but read what Job and God have to say to each other. You may recognize something of yourself.

In our search for God in the depths the words of the psalms can be a great support:

O knit my heart unto thee, that I may fear thy name. (86:11)

For innumerable troubles are come about me; my sins have taken such hold upon me that I am not able to look up: yea, they are more in number than the hairs of my head, and my heart hath failed me. (40:12)

I will come unto thine house even upon the multitude of thy mercy. (5:7)

I stretch forth my hands unto thee: my soul gaspeth unto thee as a thirsty land. (143:6)

The Lord himself is the portion of mine inheritance and my lot. (16:5)

He made darkness his secret place: his pavilion round about him, with dark waters and thick clouds to cover him. (18:11)

He shall send down from on high to fetch me: and shall take me out of many waters. (18:16)

Many passages from the Psalms could be quoted, especially all of Psalms 27 and 42, as well as much of Isaiah. Other passages from both Old and New Testaments are wonderfully strengthening in depression. But what speaks to one person will not speak to another and you have to search for yourself.

As I said, the basic urge in depression is to run away. But you cannot run away from yourself. Even suicide offers no certain end to our distress, for we do not know what happens after. The only way to go is inwards and downwards to the depths of one's own being – and God is there. For those 'who going through the vale of misery use it for a well . . . the pools are filled with water' – they are filled not only with water but with pearls of great price and buried treasure. And although I would not wish the agony of depression on anyone, those of us who suffer from it can, if we are willing, find depths there which seem in some ways to be comparable to the heights which the mystics reach. Of course, it is only when you are through the worst of the depression, at least for a time, that you realize what it has meant.

13

The way of a priest

When I read books of good advice on spiritual matters I often want to question the writer. Does he practise what he preaches? How does it work out in his own life? I must try to answer that sort of question for myself.

I was ordained in South Africa and worked there until some rather traumatic events brought me to England in 1972. In 1974 I was instituted as rector of St Vedast's in the City of London. I knew little about how the church worked here or about the City, but I was deeply thankful to be in charge of a church again. St Vedast's is a beautiful Wren building, marvellously restored after heavy bombing in the war. The congregation sit facing each other, as in a college chapel, rather than facing the altar; I think this has helped to build up a sense of relationship between the members. The Blessed Sacrament is reserved in a side chapel.

St Vedast's is one of the few City churches to have a rectory attached. I would have found it difficult to do my job without this easy access to the church and without a comfortable setting for personal interviews; yet it is an impracticable place with three steep flights of stairs up to its comfortable study. There is a large drawingroom suitable for entertaining such as few incumbents could afford, and a minute flat for the housekeeper whom I cannot afford either – although I do have people living here who look after me admirably. There is a delightful little courtyard and a good-sized parish room with a kitchen attached. These have been invaluable in building up *koinonia* within the congregation.

St Vedast's lies almost in the shadow of St Paul's Cathedral and on the edge of its own parish which has absorbed no fewer than fourteen medieval parishes. Yet we are short of resident parishioners, and those who come to services often travel from a distance. Some are attracted by the church's musical tradition, its famous organ and good cantors. I felt at first that there was not enough opportunity for the congregation to share in the spoken word and not enough silence; I do think that in some ways a really pregnant silence is more important than a sermon. Of course many church congregations find their music distracting because it is so bad rather than because it is so good; in both cases people may find themselves thinking about the music rather than about the service. But, good or bad, if it is offered to the best of our ability to the glory of God, and if the whole liturgy is offered that way, the music will take its rightful place.

Most of those who come to the church are single people, childless couples, or those whose children have grown up. Perhaps the church serves a real need in its ministry to people living alone, especially to single professional women who often find themselves rather left out in parish churches which are more centred on family worship. On weekdays we have a midday Eucharist, and on Mondays I celebrate at 8 a.m. and on Saturdays at 8.30. The weekday communicants and the Sunday worshippers form two distinct congregations.

When I came here I had to work out a routine for myself which would fit in with the midday service. I had been used to celebrating not later than 8 a.m. and I found adjustment difficult. Now, my pattern is that I set my alarm for 5 a.m. and get to church by 6.0. I begin by saying matins, I then go on to intercession. (Ever since my ordination I have believed that praying for the parish and the world is one of the most important things which a parish priest has to do, and for many years I tried to put aside half an hour for this between 12.20 and 1 p.m., to keep this time sacrosanct and to get people to understand this.) I complete my morning prayer with an attempt at the practice of adoration. This pattern is theoretical for, in practice, the sound of my alarm marks the beginning of a monumental struggle to get really awake. By the time I have opened up the church it may be 6.15 and I may suddenly wake up in Matins to find that I have snoozed off and cannot remember where I have got to in the Psalms. This often means that I cut short the hour which I aim at spending in adoration.

On both Sundays and weekdays I try to get back to church for a period of prayer before Holy Communion. I pray 'that I may celebrate these holy mysteries with reverence and love, and lovingly, with holy fear, with a perfect memory of all the words and actions, with a perfect carefulness, and with a perfect impersonality that I may not come between Thee and Those who come to receive Thee'. I can't sing well, so I pray that God will touch my lips that I may make the right sort of sound. Also on Sundays I pray that I shall preach 'as I ne'er shall preach again; and as a dying man to dying men'; and I pray that 'the Holy Spirit may go before and touch the ears and minds and the hearts of all the people who come, that the faithful may be strengthened, and those who approach Thee may find Thee and be found of Thee'. And I try, without obvious success, to 'pray people in' according to an old evangelical custom. I pray that people may come from their homes, their houses, their flats, their bedsitters, their hostels, from far and near: young and old, faithful and unfaithful, and some pagan folk brought by friends – may all who need to come, come and be reached and touched in some way.

At this time I pray for my own particular intention and for my own needs. I pray for forgiveness and the healing of the spirit. I claim healing for my depression and for my fears which are legion: fear of surgery, fear of nightmares, fear of failure and rejection. I pray for healing for my body which has been plagued by a number of ills and kept going, not only by what doctors have done for me, but through the blessing of the Sacrament given – according to the 1662 words of administration – 'to preserve thy body and soul unto everlasting life'.

In the afternoon or early evening I say Evensong. I sometimes wonder if I am a bit neurotic to hold to the discipline I was taught at my theological college. (I remember the days off at college when we gathered by the seaside to say Evensong together.) Young priests today see the offices as less of a rigid duty and are more flexible about them; but I myself regard the offices as part of the basic bone-like structure of the priesthood. I wonder whether I would ever have been ordained if I had been given the indeterminate direction which many young men receive today. The offices help us to pray even when we are feeling anti-religious. We receive the daily grounding of our faith in the Scriptures and the great canticles. To say the office is to join in the prayer of the whole Church, the worship which rises morning and evening across the world. The priest who knows that he wants to serve God should find there a fulfilment of his desire and commitment. He should find in his regular Eucharist and offices the base from which he can grow; and he will not grow if he feels, as many priests feel today, that he is left free to flounder.

It will seem to some that I speak from a ivory tower. Certainly I am not overwhelmed by the pressures of parish life or the varieties of more secular activities which can clamour for the priest's attention. I have no family and only one church to care for. I am able to try to concentrate on the things of God. My life in Africa was different, with seventeen years as dean of two cathedrals (Salisbury, then Johannesburg), and a full share of parish and diocesan administration. As Dean of Johannesburg I had to challenge the blasphemy of apartheid and found myself accused of being too involved in politics. And as a young priest I found myself in charge of a parish with seven churches. I do understand the difficulties of those who cannot pattern their prayers as I have been fortunate enough to be able to do. But the priest's own devotion and worship form the background for his work with other people. In Africa I often knew myself involved in a visible battle between good and evil, whereas in England the evil one works more subtly, inciting a self-satisfaction and spiritual laziness which is as destructive as apartheid. I think my chief job here – beyond the service of the altar – is to say my prayers and to help the small groups and individuals who have looked to me for counsel about prayer and the management of their Christian lives.

People come in all sorts of ways. Some are members of our congregations. Some knew me in Africa, some have read my books or heard me preach. Some have been referred to me by their clergy. Some come out of the blue and after one interview I never see them again. This work of spiritual guidance is a primary aspect of the priestly task, and indeed the task of any Christian who finds himself or herself called to it.

People come for all sorts of reasons: some are overwhelmed by a personal tragedy which has challenged their faith; some are agnostics who are looking for some kind of answer to the emptiness of their lives; some are facing personal tangles or are in moral confusion; some are trying to deepen their prayer life and their contact with God. One cannot foretell what people will want to talk about and one must allow time to listen. Sometimes I feel as if I have nothing worthwhile to say, yet almost always something does come out which is helpful; the other person discovers it for himself rather than from me. Even when the way out of someone's difficulties may look straightforward, it may not be wise to say so; it may not really be so simple for the enquirer who needs to work out the solution more gradually for himself.

One is constantly being asked questions of the 'Why suffering?' type. When I don't know the answer, which is very often indeed, it is worthwhile to say so and go along with people in their non-understanding. In the end the only answer, or at least the only satisfactory response, lies in our encounter with God himself. Another common complaint is that the Church seems to get in the way by its dullness, its appalling record of persecution, or its apparent irrelevance. Yet, I point out, neither I nor my visitor would be concerned about Christianity if the Church had not been there to pass on its message. It may have passed on Christ's teaching very badly – and it was partly that failure which called me into the Church: I wanted to get inside and do my bit in putting things right. I can share my own criticism of the Church and also my faith that it is a divine organism surviving despite its faults.

When people come to me to talk about the spiritual life, I try to find out where they have got to and what kind of prayer they are doing. Do they find it easy to be thankful? Are they, like many nowadays, depressed by the state of the world and its agony? What is their particular attrait, the vision which draws an individual and makes him or her want to pray? It is important to suggest some way forward in which enquirers may use their own qualities – for example, as depression gives a means of identifying with the agony of our Lord or God's pity for his world. The depressed person really has a way to God which a happy person does not have.

Sometimes a spiritual guide must be more definite. There are times when one should say firmly, 'This is wrong,' or, 'That is what you ought to do,' as Nathan spoke to David. But this demands a knowledge of the person and of the spiritual life, a spiritual discernment which I don't think I have. Evangelicals often speak to a prospective convert in black and white terms: 'If you want to serve Christ you must do this or you must not do that.' That technique did not work when it was tried on me as a youngster; but there are times when it does work.

One of the difficulties which beginners face is the insatiability of God. The more they pray, the more they find they are being taken over; they are frightened that they are going to be asked more than they can give. One must help people to recognize that they can never meet God's demands wholly and that our lack is made up by our Lord's sacrifice. And our own sacrifices are not unacceptable although they are tatty and incomplete. God does his best with what he is offered – as with the five barley loaves and two small fishes.

Christians encounter different problems at different stages of their Christian development and that is a reason why continuing spiritual direction is a good thing. Some of the traditional teachers seem to regard the spiritual life as a steady progression from the purgative way, in which the typical prayer is vocal prayer, through the illuminative way in which meditation is typical, to the unitive way marked by adoration. These are these three kinds of prayer, but I do not see them as being necessarily consecutive. Right at the beginning of our life of prayer we are given some experience of unity with God, for without it we would never get started. I think development in prayer is less like a car changing gear as it speeds up than like a spiral in which you come back and back to the same idea or glimpse of God but with a higher or deeper experience of its meaning. If one were to take the three-fold way literally, one might say that most Anglicans who are pretty deeply committed, or at least regular communicants, are at the point of changing from the purgative into the illuminative way. They are beginning to use affective prayer; that is the prayer of few words arising from the heart, words like 'Jesus', or 'Yes' or 'Love'. This kind of prayer may begin without conscious effort, at communion or after meditative Bible reading. People often need help because they are afraid of doing the wrong thing or of being too emotional, so it helps them to be shown that this is a valid and right step. I suggest one or two books of affective prayer which may help them to find words. As a young man I was helped by Shirley Hughson's *Corda in Caelo* (SPCK). Many people find help at this stage in Eric Milner White's *My God My Glory* (SPCK) or books by Gilbert Shaw (Fairacres Press, Oxford). Recently I came across *A Book of Short Prayers* by Graham Smith (Veritas Publications, Dublin). It is good for people to make their own collections of phrases which ring bells for them.

My work in teaching and guidance often brings me into contact with young priests. I think some are confused about the nature of their vocation as priests. They have been taught the techniques of counselling and running a team, and gimmicks for publicity and fund-raising. This may be good for parish or diocesan life, but it is superficial training for a man whose real work is to introduce men to God. He cannot answer people's conscious needs, or reach down into their almost unconscious yearning for God unless he himself has spent quite a long time trying to know God and to love him. He has been 'ordained for men in things pertaining to God'. When the priest is not geared this way, his people suffer and he suffers himself, and I suppose that in some way God suffers too. Many men face frustration and a sense of failure, a lack of fulfilment, because they are uncertain about their real aims.

Of course some priests who come to see me have specific difficulties, sometimes sexual ones. They may be homosexuals trying to work out how to manage their relationships. If they ask me whether homosexual relationships are right I say that, in terms of genital relationship, I personally don't think they are. But my real concern is to try to help the person who is talking to me to deal with his situation as best he can. He may feel that physical relationships are acceptable provided the partners are faithful to each other, though I think myself that this is at least doubtful. Perhaps theological colleges should do more to help individuals before ordination.

Marriage breakdowns are increasingly common among the clergy, or at least they are more commonly open. When they are openly acknowledged it does allow opportunity for competent help to be sought. The situations are often tragic and seemingly irreparable. Over the last years I have talked with priests who have divorced and remarried; some have been allowed to continue their priestly ministry and some not. I am no judge of what is right about this; my job is to try and help them in the situation in which they find themselves.

Hearing confessions is an important part of the ministry which I think ought to be kept separate from spiritual direction. I would rather people coming to confession expected absolution and some simple comment, and made an appointment at another time for a longer conversation. I know that some people feel that they do not have other opportunity to talk about their spiritual problems and some Anglican priests do give a good deal of advice in confession.

As priests we are 'ministers of Christ and stewards of the mysteries of God'. Unless we are that first, everything else comes to nothing. If I had to describe the priest's vocation in the present world I would use the words sent on a postcard to the Society of the Sacred Mission when they were working out the vocation of their house in Milton Keynes: 'Don't just do something. Stand there!' That is precisely what we are called to do – to stand there at the altar lifting the world to God and offering God in Christ to the world.

But we need the support of our people and my last word is for them. You remember how Alice, in *Alice in Wonderland*, meets the Mock Turtle who is sitting sad and lonely with his large eyes full of tears. 'Once upon a time,' he says, 'I was a real turtle.' That reminds me of one or two clergymen whom I know. They look back and think, 'Once upon a time I was a real priest. I went into the priesthood because I wanted to be a real priest.' They wanted to care for the sick and the lonely and the mysteries of God, and to minister to the poor and the outcast. Then, as the years went by they got tired and a little slack, and their prayers began to get a bit formal. They grew selfish and lazy – and that was partly your fault! There are too few of you who pray daily for your priests, and we need your prayers. Whenever we gave up whatever other career we had in mind and came into the priesthood we set ourselves a high standard. We set ourselves in the place where evil was most likely to attack us. We set ourselves in the forefront against the principalities and powers of spiritual wickedness in high places; and often we are left there alone. We need your presence at the daily services. We need you to pray for us by our names.

Postscript

I went through the great door of St Vedast's which had survived
two fires of London, and stood looking round. A stout priest
appeared. 'Can I do anything for you?' he asked. I told him
that I was just exploring and he offered to show me round. He
gave a lively account of the building and then led me out into
the little countyard. 'If ever you feel tired in the City,' he said,
'come and rest here.' I went away without learning his name.
But one thing leads to another; in time I began to learn the
answer to his question, 'Is there anything I can do for you?'

Ten years later I ask myself how I should write the postscript
to his book. I should try to bring its threads together, but they
come together of themselves as they all lead to God. I picture
different readers picking up quite different threads as they find
something which speaks to their own condition or enforces or
enriches their own personal vision. Some will find an understanding of Christian fellowship, or of some Christian belief,
or of the privileges and disciplines of priesthood. Some may
find that the author has touched their private distress. Many
perhaps will feel that they have come with him to the altar. I
have found his words most relevant when they point beyond
words and into the silences where we wait on God.

A year or two before the book was thought of, I attended a
gathering at St Vedast's and wrote an account of it in my
journal. I described a picnic lunch in the sunshine and Canon
ffrench-Beytagh standing alone in the shadow on the other side
of the courtyard. He held a glass in his hand and I noticed that
he wore the green ring which had belonged to Archbishop
Clayton. He looked white and happy and alight. Later I went

across to the church for Evensong and knelt thinking about the silence. Did the silence hang in a cloud of prayer, or the prayer hang in a cloud of silence? Were there memories of prayers clustering in the aftermath of Sunday's incense? There were roadworks in Cheapside but their clangour could not fracture the silence which seemed almost tangible. It licked round the plaster ceiling picked out in gold and silver; it drifted down the dark red hangings and round the brass lampstands on the dark stalls. What is it, I asked myself, that gives a church a sensible feeling of prayer and holiness? Then came a quiet Evensong. The Canon read the story of the death of Absolom, softly and tenderly.

'A dull day?' I wrote. 'Nothing special had happened. Nothing special had been said. But I felt, as they say, that my batteries had been charged. I had been to a place "where prayer has been valid" and – not for the first time at St Vedast's – I felt close to a gap in the hedge between here and yonder.' In his retreat talks Gonville put a similar perception more clearly when he spoke, not of a gap in the hedge, but of a thin place in the cloud which hides God's glory, and spoke of the sense of God's presence which we may feel in a church where the sacraments have been celebrated for hundreds of years. Of course, churches are not the only places where we know God's presence. Gonville clearly knew it in a high cathedral and a prison cell, at the Grand Canyon and in unexpected places 'like a back street in Cambridge'. One thing he has given me is an assurance of the validity of those moments when we seem to catch an echo or a glimpse of glory. But the teaching in this book points us beyond our own experience. Practical as his teaching is, it never loses touch with the great invisible things. We are called to join the whole of creation, and the whole Church down the years and across the world, and the whole company of heaven, in the eternal song of praise:

> Holy, holy, holy, is the Lord God Almighty,
> who was and is and is to come!

VERA HODGES